Found:
Long-Term Gains From
Early Intervention

AAAS Selected Symposia Series

 Published by Westview Press
5500 Central Avenue, Boulder, Colorado

for the

 American Association for the Advancement of Science
1776 Massachusetts Ave., N.W., Washington, D.C.

Found:
Long-Term Gains From
Early Intervention

Edited by Bernard Brown

AAAS Selected Symposium 8

AAAS Selected Symposia Series

Copyright © 1978 by the American Association for the Advancement of Science

Published in 1978 in the United States of America by

Westview Press, Inc.
5500 Central Avenue
Boulder, Colorado 80301
Frederick A. Praeger, Publisher and Editorial Director

Library of Congress Catalog Card Number: 78-3120
ISBN: 0-89158-436-6

Printed and bound in the United States of America

About the Book

Since the founding of Project Head Start in 1965, there has been intense public as well as academic debate about the effectiveness of early intervention programs in producing lasting gains in children's intellectual development. In the past few years, new evidence has accumulated at a rapid pace, and there are now over 100 major studies of longitudinal experiments and Head Start program evaluations. A series of longitudinal studies of early intervention experiments was begun in the 1960s. The children who participated in these programs are now past the third grade and old enough to give reliable responses to IQ and achievement tests. In addition, they have now been in school long enough to allow examination of their overall school performance. This volume includes reports which review both center and house-based early intervention programs. One of the papers presents preliminary findings from the Developmental Continuity Consortium which is pooling the data from 12 major longitudinal experiments.

The authors cite evidence for late developing gains which seem permanent. These "sleeper effects" were not manifest in the scores of the same groups of children in the first few years of the postintervention period. In addition to IQ and achievement gains, there is also evidence for gains in emotional adjustment. Early intervention appears to have dramatic effects in the assignment of children to special education classes and on retention in grade, somehow enabling them to maintain their position in the classroom. In all, the papers describe 96 major studies which report positive impacts from early intervention programs.

Introductory Note

The papers included in this volume were presented or referenced at the Symposium "Found: Long-Term Gains from Early Intervention" held at the American Association for the Advancement of Science meeting in Denver, Colorado in February 1977. The object of the Symposium was to examine new evidence about the effectiveness of early intervention programs such as Head Start in producing lasting gains in the intellectual development of disadvantaged children.

The Symposium participants were: Bernard Brown, Robert Hess, John H. Meier, Francis Palmer, Victoria Seitz and Virginia Shipman.

We thank Dr. Kathryn Wolff and Ms. Arleen Rogan of AAAS for their help in seeing that the results of the Symposium were published.

Contents

Introductory Note   vii

List of Tables and Figures   xi

Foreword   xv

Preface -- *Edith H. Grotberg*   xvii

About the Editor and Authors   xix

Introduction-- *John H. Meier*   1

1   The Effects of Early Childhood Intervention-- *Francis H. Palmer*   11

     Professor Martin Deutsch   21
     Professor E. Kuno Beller   22
     Professor E. Merle Karnes   24
     Professor Louise Miller   25
     Abelson-Seitz   27
     Dr. David Weikart   28
     Professor Susan Gray   29
     Professor Ira Gordon   30
     Dr. Phyllis Levenstein   31
     Conclusions   32

2   The Effects of Parent Training Programs on Child Performance and Behavior-- *Barbara Dillon Goodson and Robert D. Hess*   37

     The Content of Parent Training Programs   37
     The Effect of Parent Training Programs on Child Outcomes   48

40750

The Effectiveness of Parent
  Training Programs on Parents   70
Discussion   74
References   77

3 Long-Term Effects of Early Inter-
    vention: The New Haven Project--
    *Victoria Seitz, Nancy H. Apfel and Carole
    Efron*   79

Method   81
Selection and Attrition Effects   84
Academic Test Performance of
  Children Following Completion
  of Intervention   93
Interview Responses, School
  Grades and School Attendance   104
Discussion of Findings from
  Interviews, Grades and School
  Attendance Data   106
Acknowledgements   107
References   108

4 The Developmental Continuity Consortium
    Study: Secondary Analysis of Early
    Intervention Data-- *Virginia Ruth Hubbell*   111

Center-Based Programs   112
Home-Based Programs   117
Methodological Considerations   119
Analyses of Original Data   125

5 A Review of Head Start Research Since
    1969--*Ada Jo Mann, Adele V. Harrell and
    Maure Hurt, Jr.*   129

Introduction   129
Summary of the Findings and
  Extent of Research in
  Selected Areas   132
Summary of the Nature and Ex-
  tent of Head Start Research   145
Summaries of Individual Study
  Findings   148

6 Long-Term Gains from Early Intervention:
    An Overview of Current Research--
    Bernard Brown   169

Index   187

List of Tables and Figures

Chapter 2

Table 1:   Identification of program cohorts   42

Figure 1:   Mean pre-post gains by program cohorts,
            grouped by pretest IQ level   50

Figure 2:   Mean pre-post IQ gains by programs,
            cohorts combined   52

Figure 3:   IQ gains by program cohorts, grouped by
            pretest IQ level   54

Figure 4:   Follow-up changes in IQ level of pro-
            gram cohorts, grouped by level of
            initial gain   56

Table 2:   Predictors of program effectiveness   60

Chapter 3

Figure 1:   A summary of the longitudinal strategy
            for evaluation of the long-term effects
            of intervention   82

Table 1:   Differences between Follow Through and
            non-Follow Through children during the
            kindergarten year (low income samples
            only)   86

Table 2:   Comparison of children who completed
            Follow Through with children who left
            Follow Through (Cohort 1 only)   88

Table 3:   Comparison of non-Follow Through
           children who remained in longitudinal
           sample with those who were lost
           (Cohort 1 only)   90

Table 4:   Comparison of children who completed
           Follow Through with children who
           left Follow Through (Cohort 2 only)   91

Table 5:   Mean values on demographic variables
           and early school performance for the
           Cohort 1 low income longitudinal
           Follow Through and non-Follow Through
           children   92

Table 6:   Significance levels of one-tailed
           t-test comparisons of FT and NFT low
           income children in Cohort 1   96

Table 7:   Significance levels of one-tailed
           t-test comparisons of FT and NFT low
           income children in Cohort 2   100

Table 8:   Mean values on demographic variables
           and early school performance for the
           low income Follow Through samples
           studied since third grade   102

Chapter 4

Table 1:   Pooled Z's and significance for *t*-
           tests by number of years after treat-
           ment termination   124

Table 2:   Analysis of covariance: Differences
           between experimental and control sub-
           jects on Stanford-Binet IQ scores,
           controlling for pretest IQ   126

Table 3:   Mean differences on Stanford-Binet IQ
           scores between experimental and con-
           trol subjects in parent-oriented pro-
           grams   127

Chapter 5

Table 1:   Research on the impact of Head Start
           by year and topic across subject area   144

Table 2:   Head Start research findings by
type of report   146

Table 3:   Number of institutional changes in
each of four categories   165

Foreword

The *AAAS Selected Symposia Series* was begun in 1977 to
provide a means for more permanently recording and more
widely disseminating some of the valuable material which is
discussed at the AAAS Annual National Meetings. The volumes
in this *Series* are based on symposia held at the Meetings
which address topics of current and continuing significance,
both within and among the sciences, and in the areas in which
science and technology impact on public policy. The *Series*
format is designed to provide for rapid dissemination of information, so the papers are not typeset but are reproduced
directly from the camera copy submitted by the authors, without copy editing. The papers are reviewed and edited by
the symposia organizers who then become the editors of the
various volumes. Most papers published in this *Series* are
original contributions which have not been previously published, although in some cases additional papers from other
sources have been added by an editor to provide a more comprehensive view of a particular topic. Symposia may be reports of new research or reviews of established work, particularly work of an interdisciplinary nature, since the AAAS
Annual Meeting typically embraces the full range of the
sciences and their societal implications.

WILLIAM D. CAREY
Executive Officer
American Association for
the Advancement of Science

Preface

The effectiveness of preschool programs, such as Head Start was subjected to searching inquiry over the past ten years. The child development community was under constant pressure to provide clear data on the long term gains of preschool programs. This pressure did not come from the Federal Administration or from Congress. These two branches of the government continued to support preschool programs even when the long term gains were not yet available or indeed were denied by some evaluations, principally, the Westinghouse Study.

No one questioned the immediate gains for children in preschool programs. The data were clear and consistent on that. It was the long term aspect that was questioned. The questions and pressures came primarily from behavioral scientists who tended to use intelligence measures (IQ) as the major criterion for these long term gains. Many of these behavioral scientists seemed unable to understand that preschool programs were not merely for intellectual development but, indeed, included the development of the whole child. Head Start was legislated as the Comprehensive Child Development Program.

But even with the narrow and hasty view of many behavioral scientists, a few were holding their judgment, gathering longitudinal data, and identifying more functional criteria for assessing long term gains, than intelligence. These more functional criteria include special education placement, grades retained, low grades, problems with the law, reading and math scores, etc. Intelligence is also included but is not seen to be as critical as other criteria for determining the long term gains from early intervention.

The studies presented in this volume demonstrate that the Federal Administration and Congress have been rewarded

this past year by the now available long term gains data from
early interventions. These data have been and continue to be
analyzed, but patterns clearly underline the success of
early intervention for later performance and behavior.

A caution, however. The data are impressive. But early
interventions do not assure that the children will perform as
well as the average child in the population. The benefits of
early intervention over non-intervention are striking, but
comparison of the children in early intervention programs
with grade norms for 4th, 5th, and 6th Grades is not impressive. The children are behind the average child in the population.

So work still needs to be done to find out what patterns
of intervention, what sequence of intervention, what critical
persons contribute to further gains over time. An analysis
of the studies presented here may suggest some hypotheses to
assure that children will be able to develop continuously at
rates appropriate for their ages and abilities.

EDITH H. GROTBERG

About the Editors and Authors

Bernard Brown is a social science research analyst with the Administration for Children, Youth, and Families (formerly Office of Child Development, DHEW), specializing in the physical and mental development of children. He has conducted studies on intelligence, mathematical models of physical and mental growth, cybernetic approaches to psychological testing, early intervention, and birthweight and placentation in identical twins.

Nancy H. Apfel is an associate in research in the Department of Psychology at Yale University. She specializes in child development and assisted in The New Haven project study at The Hamden-New Haven Cooperative Education Center.

Carole Efron is an evaluation consultant at The Hamden-New Haven Cooperative Education Center in Hamden, Connecticut. Her fields of interest are psychology and special education.

Barbara Dillon Goodson is an analyst with the National Day Care Study at Abt Associates in Cambridge, Massachusetts. She has done research on observation behavior in the classroom, models of early education in cognitive and language development, and day care.

Edith H. Grotberg, director of the Research and Evaluation Division with the Administration for Children, Youth, and Families at DHEW, specializes in child development and reading and learning disabilities. She was formerly director of the Graduate Program on Learning Disabilities at the American University. She is chairperson of the Executive Committee, Federal Interagency Panels on Children and Youth and the editor of Day Care: Resources for Decisions.

Adele V. Harrell, research associate with the Social Research Group at George Washington University, worked on

*the White House Conference on Children follow-up study, and
has published a number of papers concerning data collection
and coordination in federally funded research relating to
children and adolescents. She is currently analyzing data on
drug abuse.*

*Robert D. Hess, Lee L. Jacks Professor of Child Education
at Stanford University, has done extensive research on family
and cultural influences upon learning in young children. He
was previously director of the Urban Child Center and the
Early Education Center at the University of Chicago. His
publications include* Early Education: Current Theorgy, Research and Practice *(Aldine, 1968) and* Speaking of Early
Childhood Education *(McGraw, 1974).*

*Virginia Ruth Hubbell is a research associate with the
Developmental Continuity Project, and is studying the long-
range effects of early childhood intervention programs. She
was formerly director of child development with the Governor's
Office of Education and Training in Mississippi. She is the
author of several papers and reports on early intervention
programs.*

*Maure Hurt, Jr., project director of the Social Research
Group at George Washington University, has worked in early
childhood education and research design. He is director of
support services for the Federal Interagency Panel on Early
Childhood Research and Development and the Interagency Panel
for Research on Adolescence. His recent publications concern
research funding emphasis and research patterns in federally
funded research and development.*

*Ada Jo Mann is a research assistant with the Social Re-
search Group at George Washington University. Her research
has focused on Head Start, and her recent publications are
concerned with research on infants and interagency coordination in these areas.*

*John H. Meier is director of Children's Village, U.S.A.,
a national program for abused and neglected children and
their families. He is former director of the Office of Child
Development and chief of the Children's Bureau at DHEW. His
most recent book is* Developmental and Learning Disabilities:
Evaluation, Management and Prevention in Children *(University
Park Press, 1976).*

*Francis H. Palmer is professor of psychology at the
State University of New York at Stony Brook; his main area of
interest is developmental psychology. He is on the Task Force*

on Mental Health and the Family: Infancy and Child for the President's Commission for Mental Health.

Victoria Seitz, assistant professor of psychology with the Child Study Center at Yale University, specializes in experimental child psychology. She is the author of several publications in this area, including "Social Class and Ethnic Group Differences in Learning to Read in F. Murray (Ed.), IRA Series on the Development of the Reading Process *(in press).*

Introduction

John H. Meier

In 1974 the Children's Bureau, a unit in the Office of
Child Development, issued a monograph reviewing longitudinal
evaluations of preschool programs entitled <u>Is Early Intervention Effective</u>. Urie Bronfenbrenner, the principal
investigator in charge of preparing the monograph, had some
rather pessimistic summary answers to this question. He
observed that even when intervention efforts do produce
substantial cognitive gains during the programs, these gains
erode away or "wash out" shortly thereafter. The most
deprived children seemed to benefit the least and the greatest erosion of their gains occurred shortly after their
entry into regular school. Such findings as these dis-
couraged many program developers and service providers from
investing more funds and efforts into preschool intervention
endeavors, especially since the suggestions for mounting
more adequate programs involved prescriptions for very
extensive and expensive changes regarding children and
families in the social order.

However, a few pioneers, perservering and perhaps
cockeyed optimists, have continued looking at longitudinal
studies. This AAAS symposium is designed to reveal how much
this work has progressed over the past decade or so. We
will hear from four of the outstanding pioneers on this new
frontier. They are to be congratulated for keeping the
faith in view of incredible odds against such long-term
studies which are dangerous endeavors because of:

Presented at the annual convention of the American
Association for the Advancement of Science in Denver,
Colorado, February 23, 1977.

(1) Attrition of subjects from an unstable and highly
mobile population;

(2) Funding policies which militate against longitudinal, high mortgage, research so that only the most
lithe and flexible entrepreneurs survive;

(3) Shifting social sands and public policy, all of
which reward innovative endeavors with dramatic
short term results which in turn provide political
ammunition;

(4) Some negative findings widely publicized by
critics some of whom may fear positive long-term
results;

and other aggravations too numerous or distracting to mention.

The Office of Child Development will soon release a
monograph, authored by Julie Richmond and Ed Zigler, old
friends of young children, recounting many of the unparal-
leled successes of Head Start during its first decade. They
include mention of the emergence of a "sleeper effect"
wherein significant differences are found at older ages
although none were found earlier. Vicki Shipman will elaborate on this "re-awakening effect" whereby the "washout
effect" (which means that earlier differences between
experimental and control subjects diminish with age) seems
to be reversed or at least attenuated with the passage of
additional time. More importantly, Richmond and Zigler
enumerate the many other goals of Head Start such as comprehensive health care, ensuring social competence, meaningful
parent involvement, etc., and they evaluate it in those
terms, a feat which the several critical national studies
failed to do. Head Start is an impressive health care
system for poor children for their general well being, let
alone the recent polio and measles outbreaks. Even the New
York Times recently ran an article linking impressive reading gains by elementary school children with their learning
in Head Start and other compensatory early intervention
programs which they had previously attended. This sort of
reawakening effect is cited in the wake of the national
alarm being sounded about decreasing literacy levels and
academic achievement scores (highly dependent upon reading
ability) among today's students. There is much other rich
longitudinal data now being mined by these "united mine-
workers" to yield lodestones showing the efficacy of early
intervention programs--the light at the end of long dreary
tunnels. Some of the gems being discovered are as follows:

In Ira Gordon's program, 30% of the matched controls were in special education by fifth grade, whereas only 10% of the experimentals were referred. This program thus resulted in a dollar saving which would easily pay for the cost of the program, not to mention the prevention of human waste and suffering.

That is why Glen Nimnicht and I started the New Nursery School in 1964 in Greeley, Colorado. A disproportionate number of children from low SES families which spoke primarily Spanish were being placed in special education whereas with the systematic intervention of the New Nursery School experience, these previously "Six Hour Retarded Children" were able to begin in the mainstream and to cope successfully with the public schools. And now evaluations of responsive programs, using what I have called a System for Open Learning, show desirable gains in many developmental domains over many years. Predictions of such success were deemed exaggerated and unwarranted. Today's predictions are highly conservative and scholarly and supportive of the predictions.

Of course, many critics of the public schools offer persuasive arguments for changing the schools to better accommodate the culturally-different child, including greater and more appropriate involvement of the child's family. At least part of the washout effect seems to be due to a "bulldozer effect" regression to the demeaning expectations and opportunities in many mediocre public school programs, including the intentional or at least inadvertent exclusion of their parents and family values from the school culture. But until the schools reach an appropriate pluralistic orientation, it is important to enable today's children to function successfully in today's relatively monolithic school society so that they may become the informed and impassioned shapers of tomorrow's world.

Rick Heber's Milwaukee Project is now being replicated by Jim Gallagher's group in North Carolina and to date is yielding similar dramatically positive results. The experimental children from the Milwaukee Project are continuing to do extraordinarily well in regular elementary schools whereas their controls have continued to decline to borderline and lower levels of mental retardation and special education function. This approach is highly controversial because it substitutes parent surrogates for biological mothers deemed incompetent as mothers. Joe Hunt's magnificent work with orphaned children in Teheran further underscores the plasticity of the very young child and the importance of competent parenting. The Brookline Early Education Project, conceived and initially directed by

Bud White, is providing extensive data on various degrees of
intensity and duration of intervention procedures and prom-
ises to be quite instructive regarding optimum matches for
individualizing experiences for children in need of enrichment to compensate for deprived home environments and
experiences.

OCD has recently funded a number of the nation's outstanding leaders in child development and early childhood
education to collaborate in a major data-gathering effort to
accumulate the longitudinal findings of their several
studies. Irv Lazar is spearheading this project (which is
funded by OCD and coordinated through the Education Commission of the States headquartered here in Denver) and is
presently pooling data from the ongoing longitudinal studies
launched by such illustrious investigators as Kuno Beller,
Bettye Caldwell, Cynthia and Martin Deutsch, Ira Gordon,
Susan Gray, Merle Karnes, Phyllis Levenstein, Louise Miller,
Frank Palmer (who is part of this symposium and addressing
center-based early intervention studies), Dave Weikart, Ed
Zigler and Victoria Seitz (who reported on the New Haven
Project). Sounds like a familiar litany of champions of
vulnerable children and their families, doesn't it? Some
of the preliminary highlights of the data analysis will be
reported to us this afternoon. The inferences and conclusions to be drawn from this data will be based upon as many
as 3,000 experimental subjects in some parameters.

It is most encouraging and gratifying to know that
Ed Zigler is compiling a major book about Head Start.
Moreover, there is a rich and expanding literature on Head
Start and analogous programs spurred on by its presence and
achievements. We are now aware of over 600 studies on Head
Start alone. Bernie Brown, a discussant in this symposium,
analyzed about 100 of these studies, over 90 of which report
favorable findings in a variety of developmental domains.
Several of the others, including the infamous Westinghouse
Report, contain many favorable findings. Refined data
analysis procedures plus the elimination of sampling errors
yields much more. Abstracts of many of these studies,
including doctoral dissertations, are kept at George Washington University in an information clearinghouse on child
and family development and early childhood education; Ada
Jo Mann, Adele Harrell and Maure Hurt have recently published an extensive treatise using this information resource.
Educational Testing Service is also warehousing a great deal
of data which Vicki Shipman and others are currently analyzing. I daresay that Bob Hess, who collaborated with Vicki
Shipman on several classical studies years ago, drew upon

the longitudinal data bank as he analyzed the effectiveness
of Home-Based Early Intervention Programs for this symposium.

In addition to these positive findings, the introduction and debugging of the Head Start Performance Standards,
a Head Start Management Information System, and the Child
Development Associate credentialling system all suggest that
our nation is now capable of massive expansion into reasonably fail-safe, high-quality national programs in early
childhood education and child and family development. All
we need is a national commitment and the provision of available resources.

The evidence to date indicates that knowledgeable and
skillful parenting is the most effective and economical
means for fostering the optimum development of the child.
Active participation by family members is critical to the
long-term success of any intervention program. Ideally,
intervention begins in preparation for parenthood and in
providing an adequate cultural milieu for nurturing of the
newborn infant. Large-scale Parent-Child Development Centers
(OCD's, PCDCs and PCCs), established as national experiments,
have clearly demonstrated the value of parental training in
the first years of life followed by preschool group experiences in which parent and child are involved and continue
to work closely together. Highly significant results have
been obtained not only for disadvantaged black families but
also for middle-class white families, Spanish-speaking
Mexican-American families, and families representative of
other ethnic groups. A closer look at one of OCD's research-
oriented Parent-Child Development Centers (PCDCs) for
Spanish-speaking Mexican-American children in Houston
illustrates the way in which this type of educational-social
intervention improve the functioning of children and their
families.

In the Houston Model program, social intervention con-
sists of working closely with both the mother and father of
very young children. Beginning at the age of 12 months,
frequent home visits by a bilingual worker introduce the
mother (and hopefully the father) to a number of techniques
for the enrichment of the child's growth and development
experiences. The mother is coached in her communication
with the child in order to promote intellectual and personality growth and development while establishing and
maintaining strong affectional bonds. Mothers and fathers
meet regularly several times a month in the evening to discuss their family problems and achievements, to share their
ideas and to seek advice. The family is dealt with as a

whole and the entire approach is carefully adapted to the
cultural values and milieu in which the family lives. Consequently, the parents are enthusiastic and most cooperative.

When the child is two years old, mother and child attend
a special nursery during four mornings a week where the child
is introduced to social interactions with other children in a
controlled and stimulating but playful environment. Video-
tape recordings of mother-child interactions are played back
for the mother so that she can see where she is facilitating
or inhibiting desired behavior in the child. In preparation
for the child's entering school, periodic contacts with the
family are maintained after the child is three years old.
Ideally, the child graduates into a preschool program like
Head Start in order to maintain and further develop his/her
growing and developing interests and abilities.

A model program of this type, incorporating the best
techniques from earlier experiments, is expensive, particularly when carried out as an experiment with a great
deal of research and evaluation accompanying the program.
However, the essentials of such a family development program
can be achieved without a great financial investment by using
volunteers and the heavy involvement of parents.

Nevertheless, one can rightly ask whether or not the
benefits from such a program, or reasonably approximate
variations on the theme, are worth the costs. The final
answers to this important question are not yet all available.
However, early returns from extensive evaluative research
over the past five years indicate the following few representative findings and trends when the experimental families
receiving the program are compared to similar families who
do not participate:

(1) Parent (primarily mother) benefits include:

Changes in parents' childrearing behaviors, skills,
values, and attitudes vary somewhat among models,
but are significant in all three programs. The
program effects on participating parents are
especially notable because they are congruent with
the whole body of research and theory dealing
with the relation of parent characteristics that
are causally linked with high early and sustained
levels of child development. Statistically significant differences between participating and
randomly assigned control mothers provide evidence
that participating mothers are:

- More sensitive to children's social, emotional, and intellectual developmental needs.

- More accepting of their children.

- More affectionate and warmer; using less punishment and more praise.

- More aware of causes of child distress; more skillful in allaying distress and comforting children.

- More aware of the range of individual differences among children, placing less value on stereotypic expectations for children.

- Use more, and more complex, language with the children, encouraging child verbalization more.

- Reason more with children, placing less emphasis on authority as shaper of desired behavior, praising child initiatives more and encouraging exploratory behaviors more.

- Feel less restricted and/or intimidated by childrearing and homemaking tasks; find children more interesting and enjoyable.

- Pursue own educational development more.

- Use community agencies more, and more skillfully, to meet family's and children's needs.

(2) Child benefits include:

Both pre-post and experimental-control group comparisons show the following statistical and, what is more important, real-life favorable program impact on participating children:

(a) Intellectual-language development

- Greater attentiveness, awareness and response to new and discrepant experiences in first year, followed by more exploratory behaviors in second and third years.

- Greater readiness for, and better skills in dealing with problem-solving situations.

- Greater vocalization in early months; more and more complex language skills achieved earlier in second and third years.

- Significantly higher general cognitive development as measured by Bayley Scales of Mental Development at about twenty months and by the Stanford-Binet Test of Intelligence at 36 months. (Importantly, these short-term effects are retained or extended at 48 months, while the children in the matched control group gradually fall further behind.)

(b)   Social-emotional development

- Earlier and stronger attachment to mothers, followed by earlier and stronger explorativeness; greater capacity to relate to strangers in second and third years.

- Interactions (first with mother, and later with others) are richer in texture, in vocalization, touching, smiling, proximity-seeking to share discoveries; more eye contact and verbalization from distances, etc.

- More and richer play behaviors and fantasy, shared first with mothers and then with other adults.

As the PCDC concept is further refined and programs are running smoothly, impacts on mothers' childrearing concepts and skills emerge earlier and stronger, and developmental differences between experimental and control infants emerge earlier and stronger and promise to endure longer.

Reports on the longitudinal effectiveness of similar programs elsewhere indicate that the children of trained parents (primarily mothers) or parent surrogates have excelled in general development and school achievement compared to children growing up in comparable homes where the mothers do not receive training. The gains resulting from such intervention programs are largest and most likely to endure when substantial changes occur in the entire environment of the child as well as in the quality of the mother-child interaction alone. This is what Urie Bronfenbrenner calls family-centered or ecological intervention. When adequate health care, nutrition, housing,

and general support of the family as a childrearing system
are not provided, the gains tend to fade or wash out once
the intervention program is discontinued.

I am delighted to announce that the first wave of replication of PCDC's is progressing smoothly, thanks to the
unprecedented collaboration and support of the Eli Lilly
Endowment and OCD with the coordination assistance of Bank
Street College. Moreover, several large states and other
foundations have expressed sincere interest in participating
in subsequent replication waves. Hence, the future augurs
well for this exemplary intervention effort, but more is
required, given the magnitude of need. In this regard, I
have attempted to distill the highest proof ingredients from
a number of proven programs to produce a powerful potion
which should be served throughout the country with whatever
mixes may be necessary for local tastes and, of course,
pluralistic tolerances.

I call the potion a NEIGHBORHOOD FAMILY DEVELOPMENT
CENTER and have recommended that a national network of these
centers be established. Unfortunately, space allocations
do not permit me to elaborate upon the salient features of
these centers. Permit me to close this introduction with
some reflections on a decade of early education by Joe Hunt,
whose seminal work relating early experience to later
development led to the conception, birth and maturation
of many of the aforementioned programs.

"To close these reflections, let me repeat
with modifications what I said in 1967: 'At this
stage of history, it is extremely important that
our political leaders and our voters understand
the limited status of our knowledge, under the
basis for our (increasingly) justified hopes, and
understand the need for support for research in
child development and for the development of more
adequate technology (for modifying the early
child-rearing practices of parents and) for an
early education.' (Hunt, 1969, p. 141) 'If our
impatient society--and the reasons for this
impatience are all too obvious--does not lose
hope and faith too soon, it is conceivable that
we of these United States of America could bring
a major share of the children of the persistently
poor into the mainstream of our society (but it
may take a bit longer than a generation).' (Hunt,
1969, p. 233.)"

It is more important that we now turn to the distinguished members of this panel, whose credentials I will not
recite, since what they have to present is more important
and will give eloquent testimony to their qualifications to
present it.   Each is a responsible and scholarly sleuth who
has perserveringly investigated the allegations that early
intervention has no long-term effects and will reveal and
discuss some long-term gains that have been found.

Reference

Hunt, J. M.   Reflections on a decade of early education.
   Journal of Abnormal Child Psychology, 1975, 3(4).

1

The Effects of Early Childhood Intervention

Francis H. Palmer

In the intense competition for this nation's resources the priority for children faces dwindling support. At a time when teenage crime and delinquency is the highest in our history, and when the reading level of the poor in the public schools is at an all time low, the suspicion is increasing that if Americans do not outright dislike their children at least they ignore them. We seem ready to default on the promissory note of universal education and prepared to exchange its costs for as yet unspecifiable allocations for increased correctional institutions and remedial services.

The average poor child is not deriving the benefits from schools that his middle-class peer is.

In 1974 there were two high schools in Manhattan where 100% of the students were reading at grade level or better. But there were seven public schools in Manhattan with 6,500 students where only 7% were reading at grade level or better. Eighty percent of that 6,500 were reading two years behind grade level. In New York, the term "learning disability" is applied to children reading two years or more behind grade level.

As for crime rates, the most recent Federal publication on the state of children in the country reports that while juvenile crime is rising at every age, the age group in which it is rising fastest is for children under 16.

Presently, the Federal government spends 1.1 to 1.4 billion dollars annually on a variety of children's

---

Presented at the Annual Meetings (1977) of the American Association for the Advancement of Science, Denver, Colorado.

services. In the establishment of priorities for available
resources, that money is not reserved for children. If
funded programs are discontinued, resources formerly available for children may be allocated elsewhere.

About 450 million of that billion dollars is presently
used for Headstart, which was created to enhance social
competence in disadvantaged children. Edward Ziegler, former
Director of HEW's Office of Child Development, has defined
that desired social competence as "the ability to master
appropriate formal concepts, to perform well in school, to
stay out of trouble with the law, and to relate well to
adults and other children."

Headstart is in serious trouble. When Congress next
votes on whether or not to maintain present funding, the
outcome is by no means certain.

Headstart has been under attack by those who maintain
that no evidence exists that it does any good. Usually that
attack is carried with evidence that preschool IQ's, raised
during and immediately after early childhood educational
intervention, drop back to the level of control groups before
the child begins formal schooling. Those attacks need examining, and the evidence on the effects of early intervention
needs reviewing.

Social and behavioral scientists' views about the
effectiveness of compensatory education may be roughly
grouped into three categories: (1) those who contend that
it has not worked and cannot, since through generations of
selective mating the poor have become genetically inferior,
incapable of responding to the stimulus of public education
as their middle-class peers can; (2) those who contend that
it has not worked because the few hours weekly spent in an
educational program are insufficient to counterbalance the
negative forces in the child's home and community environment; and (3) those who contend that there is evidence of
positive effects upon subsequent school performance, and
that the jury is still out on most questions related to
issues such as crime and delinquency.

The voices which ascribe a genetic basis for the
average performance of populations in the public schools are
not many but they are loud. It is an old hypothesis which
surfaced to public attention because of an article in the
Harvard Educational Review by Arthur Jensen in 1969.
Entitled "How Much Can We Boost IQ and Scholastic Achievement?", his opening sentence was "Compensatory education has
been tried and apparently it has failed." What followed was

a discussion of the nature of intelligence and argument that
IQ as measured by some traditional measures associated with
that acronym did in fact measure what intelligence is; a
review of evidence he believed supported the notion of
heritability for that characteristic based largely on Cyril
Burt's twin studies conducted with middle-class whites in
Britain and the United States; and conclusions that some
populations, particularly Blacks, were genetically inferior
with respect to the manipulation of abstract symbols and
problem solving. While only about 10% of the article had
reference to Blacks and only a little more to the subject of
scholastic achievement, what he said about Blacks appealed
to the news media and what he said about scholastic achievement was "the heritability of scholastic achievement is much
less, on the average, than the heritability of intelligence,"
and later, "The proper evaluation of such (compensatory
education) programs should therefore be sought in their
effects on actual scholastic performance rather than in how
much they raise the child's IQ." This writer for one cannot fault Jensen for presenting a hypothesis and then mar-
tialing the evidence he believes supports it, which is what
he did in the bulk of the article with respect to his definition of intelligence and the genetic basis for it.
What has been little noted in journalistic media, at least,
is the fact that he contended that compensatory education
had failed and stated paradoxically that the only measure
to be used to determine whether it worked or not was in
subsequent scholastic performance. This, in 1969, when the
vast majority of children participating in such programs
had not yet been assessed in school!

        In other places or other times the Harvard Educational
Review article would probably never have surfaced to public
attention. It would have been grist for the academic mill,
debated in small conferences and rejoined by other articles
in scholarly journals. But with this nation's sensitivity
in the late 1960's about the Blacks, and with the total
commitment to environmentalism which had provoked the
allocation of vast federal expenditures to modifying the
environmental conditions of the poor, Newsweek, The New York
Times, Atlantic, and other literate periodicals embellished
the theme of the IQ and the pros and cons of its heritability. The crucial issue posed by Jensen was lost. Does
compensatory education influence subsequent school performance? Does early intervention effect reading ability,
arithmetic competence and other school-taught skills which
presumably we still believe are related to whether or not
a child can assume a role compatible with himself and with
society?

Those who say that the amount of time the child is exposed to compensatory education programs is insufficient to counteract the devastating effects of the ghetto home and community rarely subscribe to Jensenism. Nor do they take the position that nothing can be done. Their point is that Headstart or other interventions have not been effective. Working with the child is not enough. What is needed is an all out effort to identify the ecological variables of the family and community which need to be changed for the child's good as well as for that of the family and community, and to try to change them. The devastating effects of the environment cannot be changed until the environment itself is changed.

An outstanding proponent of this position has been Professor Urie Bronfenbrenner of Cornell University, a distinguished expert on child-rearing practices. From an address before the American Psychological Association in 1974, he said, "Recently, I completed a report for a committee of the National Academy of Sciences reviewing available research on early intervention projects conducted over the past ten years. Although there were some modest achievements, by and large the results were disappointing. The effects were at best short-lived and small in magnitude, with substantial overlap in the distributions for experimental and control groups. In short, my optimism about the plasticity of the developing organism (read children) and its responsiveness to environmental change turned out to be ill founded."

And from that report to which he refers, "it is clearly evident from every project that preschool intervention is effective in producing substantial gains in IQ that are generally maintained so long as the program lasts...the experimental groups do not continue to make gains when the intervention is continued beyond one year and...one year after intervention is terminated, the IQ of the 'graduates' begins to drop, the difference between the experimental and control groups gradually decreases, the once impressive gains are reduced to a few points, and, what is most crucial, the average IQ of the experimental group often falls back into the problem range of the lower 90's and below."

So it is that these two different groups of child experts, miles apart in theoretical persuasion, have joined in concluding that working with young children to provide them with experiences relevant to subsequent school and social performance is not effective. The extent to which they have influenced decision makers cannot be specified, but that they have been heard and noted is uncontestable.

Then there are those who say there is data to show that
early intervention can influence school performance. They
contend you cannot determine the effects of compensatory
education on scholastic performance until the children
concerned get into school. Acceptable measures of, say,
reading achievement are just not available until about the
third grade, and reliable statistics on crime and delinquency are not available until the teens. Furthermore,
results available today are for those studies which used our
first approximations of what early intervention should be.
As we learn more about the developing child from basic
research, we will improve methods of early intervention.
As we learn more about delivery systems and program administration, we will more effectively bring the results of new
knowledge to bear on the individual child.

Large sums have been invested so that the effects of
compensatory education can be evaluated. The social and
fiscal climate makes it unlikely that new evaluations will
be started in the foreseeable future. These evaluations
are the only data base that exists to determine whether or
not intervention works. The children concerned are just
coming of age when school and delinquency data can be
gathered. Don't deprive the nation of its only chance to
determine what effect, if any, compensatory education has
had. Debate the merits of the research after the data are
in, but don't make the mistake of not getting it. The issue
is too important to ask the jury to reach a verdict before
all the evidence is presented.

There are a number of studies about the effects of
intervention which were designed with the careful selection
of subjects, the existence of appropriate control groups,
the precision of implementation and the sophistication of
measurement to qualify as research. Several of those have
evidence about what happened to the children involved when
they subsequently attended school. These are the studies
to which we must turn to evaluate the effects of compensatory education.

In the descriptions that follow it would be endlessly
repetitive to provide details about subject selection,
research design, and the logistics inherent in conducting
each individual study. Yet to provide a perspective within
which all of these studies must be judged, some detail about
one is needed to communicate the nature and extent of the
effort involved in each. Perhaps some detail about the
study I know best will suffice to provide that perspective.

In 1963, with funding from the National Institutes of Health, I had the opportunity to begin to investigate an aspect of compensatory education. Would minimal intervention, two hours weekly for eight months, have an effect on the subsequent scholastic achievement of children who were 24 and 36 months of age when intervention began?

On 126th Street between Charlie's Bar and the 24th Precinct Station on the one side and the Catholic school at St. Nicholas on the other, the Harlem Research Center was established. Before it was renovated for our purposes it had been a heavy machine shop, located in a second floor loft. Three hundred and ten 2- and 3-year old children climbed those stairs twice weekly for the next two years.

The children were selected from 1500 birth records of those born in the Harlem and Sydenham Hospitals between August and December of 1964. They were all male and they were all Black. Males because the developmental differences between boys and girls were judged to be a variable which if studied would have required twice the sample size, resources, facilities and staff. Blacks because the research design required children from a broad range of social class who lived in a manageable geographic area. Harlem is not all ghetto. Many of its residents are middle and upper middle class families. Each child had been over 5 pounds at birth. All had parents who spoke English as a first language. None had mothers with a history of narcotics addiction. Half were from families whose head of household was unemployed, on relief or receiving Aid for Dependent Children. The other half were sons of the employed, ranging from those minimally supported in menial jobs to a few who were by any definition upper middle class. None were what Gunnar Myrdahl described in The American Dilemma as the under-class--those children born without benefit of physician or clinic. We don't know how many of these there are in this country. By the nature of their existence they defy the census.

The 310 children who participated in the study were selected for predetermined social class criteria. That selection process required over 700 home interviews attempted and over 500 achieved. The participants were assigned randomly to three groups: 120 to be exposed to the program at 24 months; 120 exposed at 36 months; and 70 controls. The original research design required that all be assessed annually until they completed the first grade.

The children who participated each year were then assigned randomly to one of two types of intervention: a structured curriculum designed to teach simple concepts believed to be prerequisite to subsequent learning; or no curriculum or other formal training, whose members otherwise would be treated identically to the concept training group. For want of another name, they were called the Discovery group. They attended the Center on the same schedules, interacted with the same instructors and were surrounded by the same training materials. Thus, in the jargon of our trade, social class, age of intervention and type of intervention were co-varied in the research design.

The rationale for the Concept Training was simple enough. It was assumed that certain simple concepts must be acquired before more complex ones are acquired. <u>Up</u>, <u>hard</u>, <u>long</u>, <u>under</u>, and <u>same as</u> and their opposites <u>down</u>, <u>soft</u>, <u>short</u>, <u>over</u>, and <u>different from</u> are eventually learned by healthy children everywhere. The environmental stimuli conducive to acquiring those concepts are present universally regardless of culture or language. The earlier the child learned those concepts the earlier he could acquire more complex ones related to school performance.

To determine the order in which those concepts should be taught, the 120 2-year-olds were given a test to determine what proportion of them already knew each of 40 such concepts. Those which were known by the largest proportion of children were taught first (over 90% knew <u>on top of</u> at 24 months) and the rest were sequenced in the curriculum as a function of their relative difficulty.

The concepts were taught in a one-to-one teacher-child interaction twice weekly in one-hour sessions for eight months. Each child in the Training group began in the curriculum at his own level as indicated by the pre-test results. Parents were asked to accompany the child during the first few sessions and as frequently thereafter as was possible, so that they would be completely comfortable with what was occurring with their child. The Discovery group received identical treatment except that the concepts were not taught, instructors did not initiate conversation with the child but responded to him if he initiated contact by gesture or verbally. Needless to say, the investigators predicted that the Concept training group would show the most pronounced durable effects over time, the Discovery group might show some effects and both might out-perform the control group.

How does one move 120 toddlers into a training center twice weekly for one hour and get them home after their instruction without chaos and confusion? One doesn't. But with station wagons and drivers, each child was picked up twice weekly for eight months, delivered to the Center and returned to his home. The climax of chaos occurred on the hour from 9:00 to 5:00, five days a week, when eight were leaving the Center for home and eight others were arriving. From 10 minutes before the hour to the hour, 16 toddlers, instructors, drivers, parents or grandparents and assorted visitors milled around the waiting room with instructor-child and driver-child pairs getting together. Things did not always go right. Once Donald Brown came in hand in hand with one driver, only to be picked up by another and taken home five minutes later. Presumably someone else had two hours of training consecutively; hopefully with different instructors. Overall, however, records showed that 80% of all appointments were kept. The day Martin Luther King was killed and Harlem was burning it was slightly lower, but they came--and all of the staff but one was present.

At the end of the eight months of training for the 2-year-olds, they and the controls were assessed on a battery of 14 measures of cognitive, motor and perceptual performance. Both groups of participating children out-performed the controls on all measures but two. Stanford Binet IQ's for the experimental groups averaged 100. The controls averaged 92. The only difference between the Concept Training group and the Discovery group was that the former knew more of the concepts which the curriculum was designed to teach. The middle-class children performed no better than the lower-class children.

One year later these children who were trained beginning at 36 months were assessed, and those who had been trained at two were brought back and assessed again, as were the controls. The results were about the same. Those trained at three were superior to the controls on most measures. Those who had been trained at two continued their superiority over the controls a year after their training had ceased. No differences of practical significance existed between the Concept Training and Discovery groups. The middle-class children out-performed the lower class on one or two measures, but the results demonstrated that at three years and eight months those differences were not compelling.

When the children were four years and eight months old, those trained at two were two years beyond the intervention and those trained at three were one year beyond. Minor differences still existed between the participating children and their controls but the case was not strong. Co-variate analysis with IQ at age three as the co-variate demonstrated that differences existed if the sum of all measures were combined, but no differences existed on any single measure of practical importance. The intervention children in both groups had not lost much on standard measures of intellective function (e.g., two points on the IQ), but the controls appeared to be catching up. Still no differences between Concept Training and Discovery. But significant differences between middle and lower class emerged both for experimental and control children. By age four years and eight months, the effects of social class were clearly manifest in the children's performance whether they had been exposed to intervention or not.

It was 1969; research support by the federal government was harder to come by; the doubters about the effects of intervention were publicly declaiming its failure. The research review committee approved continuation of the research but funds were not available for it. Small sums were found in 1970 and 1971 to continue analysis of the data and to keep in touch with the families concerned. Assessment in the first grade never occurred.

In 1975, however, when the modal subject in the study was in the fifth grade, the Education Commission of the states provided funds to locate and assess the Harlem study sample.

As of now data exists for 233 of the 295 children (79%) who are valid subjects today of the 310 who began the study in 1964. Of the 15 children who are not considered a valid part of the study at this time, 18 did not complete the training program in 1967 or 1968, and seven were never located for assessment immediately after training nor at any time since. We have some data on 51 of the original 68 Controls (75%) and 183 of the 227 experimental subjects (80%). But complete data do not exist for all subjects.

The most complete data are for 1975, when the boys were 11 and the modal subject was in the fifth grade. We have 159 IQ's, 173 arithmetic achievement scores, and 169 reading achievement scores for that year. For each measure, the proportion for whom scores are available for control and experimental groups does not differ. For example, 1975 arithmetic scores are available at this time for 62% of the experimentals.

Attrition analysis, conducted by comparing IQ's and social class at ages three and five (the last assessment) for those found and not found in 1975, showed no significant differences between any of the groups in the design.

The mean IQ (WISC) for the four experimental groups [concept training (CT), discovery training (DT), trained at age two (T-2), and at age three (T-3)] were significantly higher than the controls (99.2 vs 93.2). Three of the experimental groups were significantly higher than the Controls: CT (p<.01), T-2 (p<.05) and T-3 (p<.025), but DT was just short of the .05 level of confidence (t=1.50).

For reading achievement the four experimental groups had higher scores than the Controls (5.01) or the Comparison group (5.0) by an average of one to four months, but only T-3 was significantly so (p<.05). Those trained at two, T-2 (5.09) were not as advanced as T-3 (5.37), but that difference is not statistically significant.

For arithmetic achievement the average child in the experimental groups (5.30) was more than six months advanced over the controls (4.68). Each of the four experimental groups was significantly more advanced than the controls (T-2, p<.05; T-3, p<.005; CT, p<.025; DT, p<.025).

And most significant of all, both with respect to the impact on the life of the boys and statistically as well, is the fact that 45% of the Controls as compared to 22% of the Experimentals are one or more years behind in grade in 1975 (x^2=11.54, df=172, p<.001).

This last finding suggests that the findings presented for reading and arithmetic are conservative. The average achievement score for the fifth grade in Central Harlem in 1975 was 5.0 and an estimated 4.8 in arithmetic. Those averages are for the boys who had made it to the fifth grade, and many do not make it along with their age group. The data presented for our sample was the achievement score obtained in 1975, whether or not the child was in the fifth grade. Thus the comparisons are between our sample in 1975, when 25% of the sample was behind one grade or more, with all of the boys in the fifth grade, many of whom had been set back as well. Rather solid evidence for the effects of early intervention, particularly when the treatment embraced only two hours weekly for eight months.

There is other evidence that intervention has durable effects on IQ scores and reading level. The studies discussed below are remarkably similar with respect to two findings. Regardless of how control groups are selected, or the locality of the disadvantaged area from which they come, they consistently show IQ scores in the low 90's and several months to years decrement in reading level. These untreated samples are the control groups with which children

given compensatory education are compared. Where early
education has been provided, regardless of the curriculum
used, durable effects on IQ and reading are more often
found than not.

<u>Professor Martin Deutsch</u>
<u>New York University, New York, New York</u>

Professor Deutsch was the first to attempt the systematic evaluation of early educational intervention and its
subsequent effects. His Institute of Developmental Studies
was formed in 1958, and shortly thereafter 62 disadvantaged
children largely from Harlem were exposed to an enriched
prekindergarten program. Three additional annual waves of
children followed, so that a total of 275 children have been
exposed to early childhood training in this study. Since
his facilities and funding could not meet the demands of all
of the parents who requested admittance for their children,
one of his control groups, 142 children, consisted of those
who applied but did not participate. A second control group
totaling 180 children began kindergarten at the same time
those who participated in his prekindergarten program did.
A third control group of 183 children was formed and consisted of children who began school in the first grade.
Varying proportions of each sample were tested through the
third grade.

His enriched prekindergarten curriculum focused on four
areas of development: language, concept formation, perceptual and cognitive and self-concept. Techniques and procedures for early learning included: designing the physical facility for a comprehensive and effective learning
environment; providing self-pacing activities and promoting
individual children's competence for learning; individualizing instruction; promoting linguistic interaction between
children and teachers; and maintaining the continuity of
instruction by carefully predetermined activities and tasks.
The scope and substance of his curricula expanded with
successive waves of children so that each did not receive
identical treatment. For later waves the intervention was
extended into the first three grades of the public schools.

While Dr. Deutsch used several measures of intellective performance at different age levels as the children
progressed through school, the Stanford Binet IQ scores and
the reading scores from the Metropolitan Achievement Test
are best compared with the other studies discussed. Perhaps
because of funding or the vicissitudes of a child's life in
the New York Public Schools, the attrition rate for his
original subjects was high. Of the original 275 children

who had prekindergarten training, data are available for 82 at the end of the third grade. A similar rate of attrition occurred for his control groups.

However, of those children who were identified and tested in the third grade, those who had received the prekindergarten training performed consistently better than the control groups. On the Stanford-Binet IQ the average score for those receiving the early training was 100 after that program was completed. By the end of the third grade that average had dropped to 97, but was still significantly higher than all three control groups, whose average was 91. The children who had received the early training and for whom reading scores were obtained in the third grade were slightly ahead of the control groups in their ability to read.

<u>Professor E. Kuno Beller</u>
<u>Temple University, Philadelphia, Pennsylvania</u>

Professor Beller asked about the effects on subsequent school performance of having begun formal schooling at the nursery level (age four), kindergarten (age five) and the first grade (age six).

His subjects were drawn from the constituencies of four public schools in an urban slum area of North Philadelphia, the family median income of which was $3,383. Parents of the four schools were informed that a nursery school would begin at each and were invited to apply if they had children of appropriate age. From those applications each school selected at random 15 children to attend. Group II in the study consisted of 53 five year olds who entered one year later the same kindergarten classes as the children in Group I, but who had no nursery experience. All children from Groups I and II were assigned in first grade classrooms when they reached that grade level so that an equal proportion of each group would have the same teachers in the four schools. Group III was selected from the first grade classrooms in which Groups I and II were, and consisted only of children who had no previous nursery or kindergarten experience. Group III children were comparable to Groups I and II with respect to age, sex and ethnicity. All three groups were kept together with the same classrooms and the same teachers through the second grade, after which they proceeded to other schools in Philadelphia according to normal procedures of school assignment. By the fourth grade, the children were distributed over eighty different schools. The study was extraordinarily successful at following the progress of the children in the third and fourth grades despite what schools they subsequently attended.

Group I, the nursery program children, were attended by a head teacher and an assistant teacher in each of the four classes of 15 children. Classes operated four days a week with the fifth school day reserved for teachers visiting homes, arranging for family contact with appropriate social agencies, and participating in an in-service teacher training program. The nursery program was traditional, with specific objectives of (a) emphasizing the need to compensate for the deprivation in the lives of the disadvantaged children, (b) helping the teacher understand the learning deficits accrued from the children's environments, (c) helping the teacher identify specific learning deficits and develop remedial learning experiences, (d) to develop specific curricula appropriate for the children, and (e) to help the teachers recognize the need to work with parents.

Standard measures of intellectual functioning and academic marks were obtained for each grade level to grade four, and a measure of impulsive and reflective cognitive styles was administered at grade four. In addition, extensive measures of socioemotional functioning were obtained.

On the Stanford Binet IQ, the remarkable consistency of scores which averaged around 90 was manifest in all three groups at the time they began schooling regardless of age. The 57 who began at age four (nursery) averaged 92; the 53 who began at age five (kindergarten) averaged 91, and those who began school first in the first grade averaged 90. Those children who began in nursery school achieved an average of 98 in kindergarten and maintained that average through the fourth grade. Those who began at kindergarten accelerated to 94 in the first grade but dropped back to their original average of 91 by the fourth grade. Those who began the first grade at 90 continued that average through fourth grade.

Academic marks showed a less consistent trend. For girls, those who began school at nursery level were consistently higher than Groups II and III in arithmetic, reading, spelling, science and social studies. Those who began in the first grade were consistently lower on those marks than those who began in kindergarten. But for boys, while those who began school at the first grade level were consistently lower than those with previous school experience for all marks, those who began at the kindergarten level were just as consistently higher than those who began in nursery school. The regularity of results for Beller's data is all the more remarkable because in the fourth grade the children concerned were in eighty different schools. In general, children who had started school earlier were more reflective than those who began later, but the results were more pronounced for boys than girls.

Professor Beller concluded from his study that "the timing of educational intervention in early childhood had immediate and prolonged effects on a wide range of the child's socioemotional and intellectual processes."

Professor Merle Karnes
University of Illinois, Champaign-Urbana

Professor Karnes asked would the Karnes Preschool Program produce greater or more lasting effects than traditional preschool programs? Her subjects were 60 4-year-old children from families in the Champaign-Urbana area who were classified as socio-economically deprived using Headstart guidelines. Two classes of 15 children each received the Karnes Program and two received traditional training. Both classes had a teacher-pupil ratio of one to five. The children in the Karnes program were subgrouped into small flexible groups of five children to one teacher daily for three structured periods of 20 minutes duration in language, mathematical concepts and science/social studies. The remainder of the 2 1/2 hours the children were in school was devoted to large group activities--music, art, directed play, rest and snack time.

The heart of the Karnes program is a special language model used to guide instruction since inadequate language patterns were thought to be the greatest problem area of low income children. A game format involving many different kinds of materials were used to encourage children to talk about their experiences. Particular attention was given to helping children develop abilities to receive, think about and communicate a wide variety of ideas.

The traditional preschool program with which the Karnes program was compared had as its goals the promotion of the personal, social, motor and general language development of the child. The teachers were instructed to capitalize on opportunities for incidental and informal learning, to encourage the child to talk and ask questions and to stimulate their interest in the world about them. Because the traditional program was implemented within a research setting, we may assume that the calibre of instruction and materials would be somewhat better than normally found in most nursery schools.

Immediate post-program effects showed that the Stanford-Binet IQ scores had risen on the average of 14 points
to 110 for the Karnes group and eight points to 102 for the
traditionally trained children. Since the national average
IQ score is around 100, and the average IQ score for poor
children at that age is in the low 90's, the immediate
effects were impressive. By the time the children had completed the third grade, about half of the original IQ gain
had been lost by the Karnes group to 103 and the traditional group to 100, a lesser loss. However, both groups
were significantly higher in IQ in the third grade than they
had been at age four, and both approximated the national
norms. Thus, while there was a decrement between the end of
the program and the third grade, the results indicated that
the children involved in both intervention groups were
higher than they would have been without intervention.

Reading achievement at the end of the third grade was
determined by the California Achievement Test, a widely used
measure for which national norms exist. The Karnes group
scores were equal to the national norm, but the traditionally trained children were lower than average. While Karnes
did not include a group of children who had no intervention
at all in her study and for a variety of reasons control
groups frequently increase in their performance, Karnes
concluded on the basis of comparisons with the national
norms that a lasting effect had been made on the children
exposed to her carefully designed program and that the
traditionally trained children evidenced positive effects
though not so pronounced.

The social relationships of children in the public
schools contributes greatly to the child's success. A
follow-up study of children in both of the above programs
revealed that children from the Karnes group were more
socially accepted than children from the Traditional group.
In addition, the Karnes children indicated that their
teachers valued tham more highly than did the Traditional
group.

Professor Louise Miller
University of Louisville, Louisville, Kentucky

Professor Miller compared the benefits of four established preschool programs. There were 248 children
involved in the study who participated in Headstart or had
no prekindergarten experience. All were from one of four
socioeconomically disadvantaged areas of Louisville which
were characterized in the 1960 census as being from 45% to
85% Black with an unemployment rate at that time of 7.5% to

12.5%. Thirty-four children, 22 of which were on the Headstart waiting list, and 13 from the same areas, had no
intervention and served as controls. The 214 others
involved were randomly assigned within areas to one of four
interventions.

The four programs she studied were: Montessori,
Bereiter-Engelmann, DARCEE, and a traditional nursery school
program. All but Montessori assume various motivational and
experimental deficits and emphasize linguistic development.
Montessori differs sharply from the other three. It assumes
that the child, disadvantaged or not, is naturally curious,
eager to learn and capable of intense concentration. All
but the Traditional program involve the careful sequencing
of tasks and a highly academic content. The Traditional
program emphasizes emotional needs, DARCEE the development
of aptitudes and attitudes, Bereiter-Engelmann the development of academic skills through rigorous drill, and Montessori focuses on long-term cognitive development. The
Traditional program and Montessori are child-centered and
individualized while the other two recommend didactic instruction in small groups.

From September, 1968, to June, 1969, the children
participated 6 1/2 hours daily, with one hour for napping
and other periods allocated for outdoor activities, lunch
and snacks. The effects for all four programs were measured
at the end of the program and annually thereafter until 1972
when the children had completed the second grade.

Most measures of behavioral change showed significant
gains for all four programs over the controls at the end of
the programs. Particularly, the Bereiter-Engelmann children
led with respect to cognitive and academic performance, the
DARCEE program made its maximum impact on motivation and
attitude change, the traditional program related to the
highest scores on measures of curiosity and social and
verbal participation and Montessori goals were reached in
two areas with high scores on inventiveness and curiosity.
In general, the immediate effects of the four programs
showed that each had achieved its goals over the control
group to one degree or another.

At that time the IQ scores of all four experimental
groups were consistently higher than those of the controls.
By the end of the second grade, however, all four groups
dropped sharply--with girls scoring lower than boys. Scholastic performance in the first and second grades was
measured with the California Achievement Tests, which includes subtests for both reading and arithmetic. At the

first grade level all four interventions yielded higher
reading scores when compared with the controls. In general,
however, those advantages for the experimental groups no
longer existed at the end of the second grade. The Montessori children were slightly but not significantly ahead of
the controls in reading, but DARCEE and traditional were
actually lower. On arithmetic, what few advantages the
experimental children had had at the first grade level no
longer existed, except that boys involved in the Montessori
program were better. Dr. Miller concluded that different
programs had different effects and that the characteristics
of each program related to its effects must be identified
so that appropriate sequences of experiences can be designed. As the programs now exist, no compelling case can
be made for any one.

Abelson-Seitz, New Haven Project
Yale University

Drs. Abelson and Seitz have had quite different results
than Professor Miller's in a slightly different context. In
1967 they began a study of children who had just completed
Headstart and who were enrolled in a special continuing
program (Project Follow Through, in Hamden, Connecticut).
The control children, some of whom had had Headstart and
some of whom had not, were enrolled in inner-city kindergartens in New Haven. Both the intervention and control
children were tested when they completed the third grade, at
which time a new group of third graders drawn from the same
school systems were tested as well.

"Results indicated that positive effects of Headstart
existed at the end of kindergarten and first grade for both
those children who had received the continued intervention
of Follow Through and those who had not. At the end of
third grade, effects of Headstart were no longer found for
those children who had been attending inner-city schools
since the Headstart experiences. Children who had received
Headstart and Follow Through intervention, however, scored
significantly higher than did control children on measures
of academic achievement, IQ, and social-emotional development."

When their sample was tested three years later in the
sixth grade, 42 children who had had both Headstart and
Follow Through continued to out-perform the same 26 control
children on IQ, general information scores and mathematics
achievement.

In 1968 they essentially repeated the above study with a
new class from Headstart. Results from the second cohort
are a little different. The intervention group did not show
superiority over their controls at the end of the third
grade. At the end of the <u>fifth</u> grade, however, the children
with Headstart experience were again superior to their
controls on three of five measures of academic achievement:
reading recognition, spelling and general information.

That finding suggests delayed positive effects ("Sleeper effects"), where differences are found at older ages when
none were found earlier. They concluded that "the evidence
points to the conclusion that the gains accruing from compensatory education programs are commensurate with the
duration and amount of effort which are expended on these
programs." They may well have added that gains also may
depend upon the age at which intervention is introduced, as
some of what follows will indicate.

<u>Dr. David Weikart</u>
<u>High/Scope Educational Research Foundation</u>
<u>Ypsilanti, Michigan</u>

The Ypsilanti (Michigan) Perry Preschool Project was
among the first studies designed to determine the effects of
early intervention with the disadvantaged child. From 1962
to 1967, 123 children three and four years of age participated in a cognitively oriented program; an equal number of
controls had no intervention except for annual testing.
Both groups entered the Ypsilanti public schools at age five
and were assessed annually thereafter on various measures of
intellective performance and on scholastic achievement.

During the program and immediately after it the difference between experimental children and their controls was
dramatic (e.g., 12-point differences in the Stanford Binet
IQ), but once treatment had terminated and the children
entered elementary schools the magnitude of those differences diminished. After the first grade no differences
remained on the Binet, and teachers did not rate experimental children significantly higher for academic potential.
However, the experimental children did consistently out-
perform their controls on the California Achievement Test,
measures of reading and arithmetic achievement. Dr. Weikart
concluded that while the initial gains shown as an immediate
effect of preschool were not sustained, "the preschool experience prepared experimental children to cope more effectively with the demands of school."

Weikart used one measure of scholastic performance with such uncontestable face validity that one wonders why more studies do not include it among assessment of effects. What proportion of the experimental and control children were actually participating at the grade level conventional for their age? By the end of the fourth grade 83% of the children who had attended preschool were at conventional grade level as compared with 62% of the controls.

Professor Susan Gray
George Peabody College

The Early Training Project was conducted in 1962-64 with 88 families who lived in two small communities in Tennessee. In one community the three- and four-year-old children in those families, whose average income in 1963 was $1,700, were randomly assigned to three groups, two inter- vention and one control. In the other community, the distal control group consisted of families with similar demographic characteristics. The program for the first preschool group consisted of three 10-week periods for three successive summers of intervention in a classroom situation, plus weekly home visits during the intervening months between one summer session and the next. The focus of the home visits was to enable the parent to become a more effective teacher for her child. The second intervention group had two summer sessions and one year of intervention in the home. When children entered the first grade, the homes were visited twice monthly until the end of that year. Assessment oc- curred immediately after the children finished the program in 1965 and in 1966 and 1968 when the children had completed the fourth grade.

Dr. Gray reports "The experimental children, as com- pared to the two control groups, showed clear evidence of superiority on intelligence tests, language tests and on school achievement through the second grade. At the end of the fourth grade, the last time the children were studied, there was still a significant difference on intelligence tests but the differences on (school) achievement data, while in the predicted direction, were no longer (statis- tically) significant." She concludes by pointing out that most of the children in the sample attended segregated schools through the fourth grade, where "expectations for the children tended to be relatively low," and that the schools have been desegregated since. She suggested that the quality of the school that children attend following early intervention is an important variable when the effects of intervention are examined.

Professor Ira Gordon
University of Florida, Gainesville, Florida

Professor Gordon asked whether systematic interaction with mother and child beginning at birth has durable impact on cognitive development. His subjects were 204 children born in Gainesville and nearby towns between June 1, 1966, and November 1, 1967. All were recruited from families which met Office of Economic Opportunity guidelines for eligibility for its programs.

His study varied duration of intervention (one to three years) with treatment beginning at birth and ending at age 36 months. The intervention was characterized by weekly home visits to mother and child at which time maternal instruction and educational procedures and materials were disseminated and by the use of women, as parent educators, who were indigenous to the same poverty-stricken population. Emphasis during the year after the birth of the child was on the development of materials and procedures which were delivered to the family on a weekly basis by the parapro-fessionals. The second year had similar goals except that the delivery system made available to the mothers provided content appropriate for ages 12 to 24 months. Intervention in the third year continued the weekly home visits and provided in addition seven "backyard centers," each located at the residence of a participating family and especially equipped for the activities in which the children would be involved. The children attended the centers in groups of five, twice weekly for four hours during which they were involved in instruction and group activities.

More than most studies, Gordon's was concerned with the spacing of intervention through time. His experimental groups consisted of families who participated all three years, the first and second two, or first, second, or third year only. Fifty-five of the 204 families involved re-ceived no intervention and served as controls.

All children were assessed annually at ages 24 months through 72 months on several measures. Only the Stanford Binet IQ is relevant here. Their performance at age six is the latest data available.

On the average children whose families received the intervention all three years, the first two, or the third year only, had significantly higher IQ's at age six than the control group. At that time the 41 controls available averaged 90.2, a representative finding for that age among disadvantaged children, and the 67 children in the three experimental treatments averaged IQ's of 98. None of the other experimental groups, intervention at 12 months only, intervention at 24 months only, or intervention in the first and third year were significantly better than their controls.

Dr. Phyllis Levenstein
Family Service Association of Nassau County,
and the State University of New York at Stony Brook

Dr. Levenstein asked the question in her Verbal Inter-action Project whether increasing the level of conversation and communication between mothers and children age 20 to 43 months of age would effect the cognitive and socioemotional growth of the children. The families concerned lived in Nassau County, New York, and are described as educationally disadvantaged because of poverty. The most recent data available are for 65 children who received two years of intervention, 39 who had earlier and shorter versions of the intervention and for 55 matched for socio-economic status but who had no intervention at all.

The intervention, called the Mother-Child Home Program, consisted of two, 1/2 hour visits to the home each week for seven months each year over two years. Using toys and books which required someone else's interaction with the child for full enjoyment and learning rather than those which provoke solitary play, the home visitor encouraged mother-child interaction with the toy. The visitor, called a "Toy Demonstrator," modeled for the mother activities which emphasized giving information about color, size and form, manipulations such as matching and building, eliciting responses from the child through questions and rewarding independence and curiosity. Illustrated books were always used with special reference to obtaining from the child questions about the pictures. During early sessions the Toy Demonstrator was the primary participant with the child, but had as her goal the eventual shifting of adult-child interaction entirely to the mother. The toys and books were permanently assigned to the child, to encourage post-program interaction. Dr. Levenstein's goal was to help low-income families assume the same educational function which many middle-class parents carry out informally in the raising of their children.

Successive cohorts of 21 (1968), 23 (1969) and 21 (1970) were in the second, first, and kindergarten grades as of the end of the 1974 school year. The average IQ for all of those children is now between 107 and 108, while 55 control children attained an average of about 92. Since

both experimental and control children when they entered the
program averaged in the low 90's, the data indicate that
those receiving Levenstein's treatment were 10-15 points
above their original scores and the controls were about the
same.

The reading and arithmetic achievement for experimental
and control children on an achievement test with national
norms showed similar differences between them. There are
also indications that the experimental children are having
fewer problems in school than the controls. From teachers'
judgments and school records the experimental children are
having significantly fewer academic and behavioral problems
in school.

Conclusions

The ten studies described involved over 2,000
children in various experimental and control groups, most of
whom have been followed through grade three or beyond by the
investigators concerned. They represent several million
dollars worth of research funded by federal agencies. No
new research of such magnitude has been funded in the 1970's.
Many of those studies were not actively following the
subjects of their research in the early 1970's. Yet they
are the primary data base for decisions about the value of
compensatory education.

In general, the results so far show that the initial
gains in IQ scores obtained immediately following the
termination of an intervention are decreased before the
child enters school, if intervention is not continuous. The
Miller study shows that those initial gains may disappear
entirely. Those preschool results were available to reviewers earlier than the evidence related to school achievement
was, and presumably it is why Jensen, Bronfenbrenner and
others decried the effectiveness of compensatory education.
Where school-age results are available, they are consistently encouraging. IQ scores, if not as high as they were
immediately after intervention, appear to be higher than
they would have been without intervention. Scholastic
achievement in reading appears to be better, and in some
cases the percentage of control children with academic
problems is reported to be greater than their experimental
peers.

Admittedly, there are questions about each of these
studies which social and behavioral scientists must examine
carefully before the results are unequivocable accepted.
As attrition occurred in the experimental and control groups

between the beginning of a study and the latest age of evaluation, is there bias in who remained available? Were the
experimental and control groups matched for intellective
levels in the first place? Did those who did the assessing
know which children had received the intervention and which
had not, and if they did, was there bias in the administration in the tests or in the collection of school data? Any
of these could effect the differences found in an individual
study. The fact remains that most studies which have evidence on effects to the school age show that compensatory
education has contributed to school performance, regardless
of the type of treatment, the age at which intervention
began, or the frequency or duration of treatment.

As to the philosophy, duration, age and intensity of
treatment, the evidence is only suggestive as to which is
best. Karnes, Miller, and Palmer varied philosophies of
treatment and their results provide little or no evidence
that one treatment is better than another so long as age
and duration of treatment are held constant. The answer to
that question may be that some children respond best to one
and others to another. Research has not progressed beyond
the randomization of assignment to treatment and control
groups to determine the effects on the average child.
Presently, there are no studies which deliberately assign
children to one or another treatment on the basis of the
characteristics of the child or his background.

As to the age when intervention first occurs and how
long it lasts the evidence suggests that the earlier and
longer the better. Gordon and Levenstein demonstrate
effects from intervention at infancy; Palmer at 24 months.
The work of Abelson and Seitz, Beller and Deutsch suggests
that intervention beginning at age four, the prekindgergarten
year, is effective if continued during kindergarten and the
first two grades. On the other hand, continued education
up to and during the school years appears to be desirable
but not essential. The Harlem study shows that two hours
weekly at age two or three can be effective without subsequent treatment before the children go to school.

Those studies which emphasize individualized instruction in the home or in a Center seem to show effects more
consistently then those in which intervention occurs in
small groups. This is not new nor is it surprising. Mark
Hopkins spoke of the educational benefits of an adult and a
child on a log in the woods. We all know that even as
adults certain insights are acquired best in the one-to-one
context. A question for research is what can be taught as
efficiently in groups as in the intimate association of two

persons alone. The significant other is an important aspect
of everyone's environment, but for what kinds of learning it
is most important we do not know.

Whether the mother or the family is involved in the
intervention is almost certainly a compelling variable with
respect to effects. Of the studies cited, Gordon's and
Levenstein's have made that interaction a principal component. That component is, of course, related to the point
that Bronfenbrenner makes. To the extent that we can influence the family with respect to behaviors related to
child rearing we will make a more pronounced effect on all
children. Few social and behavioral scientists would argue
with that. One can even agree with Bronfenbrenner that
identifying those aspects of the child's ecology relevant to
his development, and changing them, would be the best of all
possible worlds. It is with respect to his saying that
intervention with the child alone has not been effective
that we are, quite literally, throwing the baby out with
the bath.

Type, age, duration, and intensity of intervention and
the extent to which families are involved in it are crucial
questions in the compensatory education picture because they
are so closely related to cost. The longer intervention
must last to be effective, the more hours per week the
child participates, the extent to which individual instruction is essential, and the added benefits from having
families involved--are all factors which will determine the
ultimate cost of national programs if they are to continue.
All of these issues are not going to be resolved by
existing research because present studies are not designed
to answer them even if they are allowed to continue. But
existing research is related to the central issue presented
at the beginning of this paper. Is compensatory education
of value?

The weight of evidence available at this time is
positive. One may criticize research design, selection of
subjects, attrition, or other aspects of an individual
study, but the fact remains that most have found positive
results and continue to do so. Thanks to the Education
Commission of the States, which with HEW's Office of Child
Development in 1976 provided funds for all of the studies
in the elementary grades--the evidence is mounting for
durable effects on scholastic achievement.

With few exceptions these results are not directly
related to Headstart. The interventions studied are not
identical to many Headstart programs. There are, however,

similarities between the interventions studied and the average Headstart program, and data were increasingly available which deals specifically with Headstart itself.

The knowledge accumulating from intervention programs can be used to make Headstart more effective with respect to subsequent scholastic performance. And Headstart does much more than provide varying degrees of educational input. It provides hundreds of thousands of preschool children with dental and medical care and a minimal level of nutritional sustenance. Those noncognitive benefits are subjects about which Headstart's critics have been noticeably mute.

We cannot give up on early intervention as one strategy to reduce some of society's malignancies. We are faced with the almost certain spectre of huge costs associated with remedial programs and expanded correctional institutions. If our angry and uneducated youth continue in the direction they appear to be going--what option do we have to early intervention and the continued accumulation of knowledge so as to make intervention more effective?

The evidence is that compensatory education has not failed. To the contrary, the evidence is that it is a healthy child which needs continued support to reach maturity.

The Effects of Parent Training Programs on Child Performance and Parent Behavior

2

Barbara Dillon Goodson and Robert D. Hess

The Content of Parent Training Programs

Programs designed to train mothers to teach school-related skills to their young children have proliferated rapidly in the decade since Head Start was first funded. The scope of these efforts varies greatly, from the federally funded Home Start program operated by the Office of Child Development with sixteen programs each serving about eighty families, to nonfunded programs run locally by volunteers. The extent of this movement is not documented and probably cannot be, but on the basis of informal evidence gathered in the course of this review, it is likely that hundreds of preschool programs exist in which parents are given some training to be teachers of their own children. A number of these programs have been evaluated. This is a review of the results of these evaluations.

Parent-centered educational programs for young children are only one form of parent participation in prekindergarten education. Others are: (1) parents as policy makers (sometimes called "community control" or "parent control"), (2) parents as supporting resources for the school in the form of volunteer aides, cleanup or maintenance groups, etc., and (3) educational activities that presumably provide parents with knowledge of child development or parenting in order to improve their competence as parents. These categories of parent activity follow closely those proposed by Gordon (1968). Although these types of parental involvement are central to many programs and are in some instances included in legislation covering state or national programs, they are not included in this review.

Programs that try to assist parents to become better teachers specify desirable new parental behaviors which are intended to support increased cognitive and social develop-

ment of children. Parents are considered crucial in the
child's development, and direct efforts are applied to parental behavior as a way of reaching the child. Education is
brought into the family relationships. These programs invoke
an implicit standard of parenting that is considered most
likely to produce intelligent, well-adjusted, academically
successful children.

Some Historical Comments About
Parent Education

Efforts to educate parents are not unique to the 1960's
and 1970's. Studies of the history of parent education
(Brim, 1959; Sunley, 1955; Schlossman, 1976) show the idea to
be an old one. As early as the eighteenth century (Brim,
1959), reports of child-rearing advice were communicated to
mothers through pamphlets. Organized mothers' groups existed
previous to 1820 (Sunley, 1955). These groups, called Maternal Associations, met to discuss child-rearing problems. The
women were usually Protestant-Calvinist mothers who were concerned about the religious and moral education of their children. The middle-class status of the women involved has been
a feature of parent education in the United States through
most of its history. These early efforts in parent education,
however, were characterized by a religious bias and ideology
of child-rearing which reflects their time period.

In the late 1800's, three national groups developed that
greatly increased organized efforts in parent education: The
American Association of University Women, the Child Study
Association of America, and the National Congress of Parents
and Teachers. All these groups attempted to educate parents
in child development to help them become more effective child-
rearers. Mothers themselves were instrumental in forming the
Child Study Association. As with Maternal Associations, the
parents themselves sought education on child-rearing, looking
to professionals for assistance rather than depending on self-
education. During the early 1900's, professional groups also
initiated efforts to offer education to parents. The National
Congress of Parents and Teachers, for example, was formed by
philanthropists, religious and political leaders who expressed
a desire to stimulate parents to learn more about child-
rearing. The efforts of the three national organizations
typically reached middle and upper-class women. The NSSE
Yearbook of 1929 stated that the parent education programs at
the time were not remedial programs for underprivileged families but were "supported by parents already giving thought-
ful consideration to training" (NSSE Yearbook, p. 276). Participation of underprivileged mothers was through the settle-
ment houses being established during the same period.

Both Brim and the writers of the NSSE Yearbook indicate that the period 1925-1935 was one of expansion of interest in parent education (and with early education). By 1920 there were over seventy-five major organizations conducting parent education programs. These included national private organizations, university-based research programs, teachers' colleges, state departments of education and vocational education, public and private school systems, social agencies, child guidance agencies, health agencies, and religious groups (Brim, p. 328). In a bulletin from the United States Bureau of Education, Mary D. Davis (1927) expressed the emerging identity of the field: "Parenthood is becoming a real profession."

The focus of parent education efforts changed between 1820 and the present. In the nineteenth century, the central interest was in children's moral and religious development. In the twentieth century, the focus shifted to children's emotional and personality growth, then included physical health, and ultimately mental health. The most recent and still current phase of parent education is organized around cognitive growth. This emphasis on cognitive and school-related behavior was not evident until the early 1960's. It was developed with the educational needs of low income children in mind. Nonetheless, middle-class parents continue to be major participants in parent education efforts. Even the concern with developing skills that would prepare the young child for successful school performance has not been confined to programs designed for low-income parents. Major public media corporations offer education-oriented records, toys, magazines, and television programs oriented toward middle-income families.

The parent participation programs reviewed here, however, are those that define low-income families as the target population and increased cognitive development and school achievement for the children as the goals. These programs are another expression of the compensatory education movement.

The Characteristics of the Program

Parent training programs have several features in common. They are developed by professionals for the purpose of instructing parents in techniques for preparing their own young children in school relevant skills. The twenty-eight programs included in this review employed several different methods for instructing parents. One method of working with parents was direct, didactic teaching. This approach was used most often in one-to-one sessions between a teacher (paraprofessional or professional) and a mother. The teacher usually instructed the mother in specific techniques to use

with her child. A less didactic method for presenting new
teaching techniques was demonstration: Mothers were expected
to learn by watching while the teacher interacted with the
child. A third method for changing parents' teaching techniques was observation in preschool classrooms. By observing trained teachers at work, parents were expected to learn
about teaching; by observing their own child, parents might
gain knowledge about the child's development, learning, and
personality.

A common feature in many parent teaching activities was
an emphasis on the use of educational toys and materials to
generate stimulating parent/child interaction. Many programs
provided toys and books to mothers or helped mothers construct
educational stimuli out of materials around the house. In
addition, programs often provided information about child
development, health and nutrition, or community resources.

The twenty-eight parent training programs (Table 1) were
identified from several sources: ERIC Clearinghouse (a computer information retrieval facility), bibliographies of parent participation and compensatory education programs,
references included in evaluation reports, and correspondence
with staffs of projects or agencies known to be involved in
efforts of this kind. Two criteria guided selection. One
was the availability of an evaluation; the other was the ade-
quacy of the information on the working details of the program.

Beginning in the spring of 1973, staff members of each
program were contacted to solicit current evaluation data.
No new reports were considered after fall, 1974. Each of the
programs were described in terms of working details, evaluation plan and results, in an earlier monograph (Goodson and
Hess, 1975). Program sponsors were invited to review these
descriptions, which were then revised in response to comments
and criticisms.

Assumptions Underlying the Programs

The developers of most of these programs share several
assumptions about educational intervention and parent involvement. The first, which we call the home deficit assumption,
is that the home in a low income community often is an
environment that fails to prepare the young child adequately
for successful entry into the first grades of public school.
This assumption is based on research showing that lower class
or lower income homes are different from middle class homes
on a number of variables presumably significant in a child's
development, such as type and pattern of stimulation, lan-

guage style, pattern of parent/child interaction, motivation, etc. The research results, however, are not unequivocal and are still the subject of much controversy.

The second assumption, drawing from research on critical periods in development, is that the early years are particularly important in setting the pace and direction of cognitive growth. The choice of preschool children as the target population is often justified by citing research on intellectual development which claim that a child's intellectual standing relative to peers is predictable by age four (Bloom, 1964). Program sponsors cite research showing the rapid development of important intellectual functions, such as language ability, during the preschool years. Consequently, it is assumed that intervention in the cognitive and language development of low income children would have maximum effect during the period of the most rapid and important changes-- the preschool years (Hunt, 1967).

The third assumption is that the impact of the family is not usually overcome by later schooling. This belief is drawn from research which shows that the family has a major effect upon the educational outcome of children, especially in comparison with the impact of differential resources in different schools (Coleman, 1966; Hess, 1969; Jencks, 1972). The influence of the family is not, it seems, greatly modified by experience in school. These reports help support the argument that the most effective channel for boosting school performance of children is through intervention in the family when the child is relatively young. Parents whose own educational opportunities were limited might benefit, and thus assist their own children, by becoming involved in programs to train them as teachers of their own children.

These three assumptions represent a particular period of thinking in compensatory education. Most of the programs reviewed in this paper were initiated in the middle and late 1960's, at a time when the concept of intervention in the homes of low income families was accepted as an effective way to equalize opportunities for children. More recently, in new programs that have been developed and in modifications of older programs, the assumptions and approach have changed. Some program sponsors prefer to consider themselves as "facilitators" rather than as "interveners." They attempt to help parents identify their own goals and then help parents plan and implement appropriate educational programs with their children. The educational interchange between parents and professionals seems to be moving toward a sharing process, away from didatic intervention.

TABLE 1

Identification of Program Cohorts[1,2]

Mother-Child Home Program (A)[3]

1. 2 year home visits

2. 1 full year + 1 short year home visits

3. 1 full year home visits + 1 year modified ("partial") home visits

4. 1 year home visits -- age 2

5. 1 year home visits -- age 3

6. comparison 2-year-olds

7. comparison 3-year-olds

8. comparison 4-year-olds

---

[1]See bibliography for program sponsors and references.

[2]"Cohort" is a single treatment or comparison group within a program.

[3]Capital letters indicate programs; numbers indicate cohorts.

Table 1 (continued)

Houston Parent-Child Development Center (B)

1. home visits -- one-year-olds

2. comparison one-year-olds

3. Center program for mother/child pairs --
   2-year-olds

4. comparison two-year-olds

First Generation Mother Study (C)

1. home visits

2. comparison group

Infant Intervention Project

Second Generation Mother Study (D)

1. home visits by professionals

2. home visits by paraprofessionals professionally-
   supervised

3. home visits by paraprofessionals supervised by
   paraprofessionals

4. comparison group

Study of Intrafamily Effects (E)

1. maximum impact group -- classes for children
   and for mothers

2. curriculum group -- classes for children

3. home visitor group -- visits to mother/child pairs

4. home visitor group

5. comparison group

Table 1 (continued)

Ypsilanti-Carnegie Infant Education Project (F)

    1.   structured home visits

    2.   unstructured home visits

    3.   comparison group

Early Child Stimulation through
Parent Education Program (G)

    1.   3 years of home visits: E/E/E

    2.   2 years of home visits: E/E/C

    3.   2 years of visits: C/E/E   (Each cohort partici-

    4.   2 years of visits: E/C/E   pated for three

    5.   1 year of visits: E/C/C   years, with system-

    6.   1 year of visits: C/E/C   atic patterning of

    7.   1 year of visits: C/C/E   experimental (E) and

    8.   comparison group: C/C/C   control (C) status)

Three Home Visiting Strategies (H)

    1.   home visits -- focused on maternal stimulation
        of cognitive development

    2.   home visits -- visitors worked with child on
        cognitive tasks

    3.   home visits -- focus on maternal stimulation of
        sensory-motor skills

    4.   local comparison group

    5.   comparison group in neighboring region

Birmingham Parent-Child Development Center (I)

    1.   Center activities for mother/child pairs

    2.   comparison group

Table 1 (continued)

New Orleans Parent-Child Development Center (J)

    1.   Center activities for mother/child pairs

    2.   comparison groups

Parent-Child Course

Mothers' Training Program (K)

    1.   training classes for parents (without children)

    2.   comparison group

Home-Oriented Preschool Education (L)

    1.   Demonstration Site I -- TV program + home visits + preschool classes for children

    2.   Demonstration Site II -- TV program + home visits + preschool classes for children

    3.   Demonstration Site III -- TV program + home visits + preschool classes for children

    4.   comparison group

Early Training Project (M)

    1.   3 years of summer preschool classes + winter home visits

    2.   2 years of summer preschool classes + winter home visits

    3.   local comparison group

    4.   comparison group in neighboring region

Special Kindergarten Intervention Program (N)

    1.   kindergarten + SKIP classes + home visits

    2.   kindergarten + SKIP classes

    3.   kindergarten-only comparison group

Table 1 (continued)

Ypsilanti-Perry Preschool Program (O)

    1. preschool classes + home visits

    2. comparison group

Ypsilanti Curriculum Demonstration Project (P)

    1. cognitive curriculum

    2. language curriculum

    3. unit-based, nursery school curriculum

    4. cognitive curriculum

    5. language curriculum

    6. unit-based curriculum

Spanish-Dame Bilingual Education Program

Ypsilanti Early Education Program (Q)

    1. classes for children + activity-oriented classes for parents

    2. classes for children + lecture-discussions for parents

    3. classes for children; parents unavailable for activities

    4. classes for children; parents refused to join

    5. classes for children + home visits + small group parent meetings

    6. classes for children + home visits to parents

    7. classes for children + home visits to child only

Programs from the University of Hawaii Center for Research in Early Childhood Education (R)

Program I -- 1967

Program II -- 1968-69

Table I (continued)

Program III -- 1970-71

1. language/motivation curriculum components in preschool classes

2. motivation parent participation

3. quantitative/motivation curriculum components

4. motivation curriculum component

5. parent participation/quantitative curriculum components

6. language/quantitative curriculum components

7. quantitative curriculum component

8. all components combined

Learning to Learn Program (S)

1. preschool classes for children + parent meetings

2. comparison group

Structured Language Program

Parents Are Teachers Too (T)

1. developmental language group -- home visits focused on maternal stimulation of language development

2. structured language group -- home visits focused on maternal teaching of specific language patterns

3. traditional parent education

4. comparison group

Teaching Parents Teaching

Project Early Push (U)

1. preschool classes + parent participation as aides, observers

---

Plan of the Review

The summary of evaluation results is organized by three major topics: the immediate and long-term effects of individual programs; the contribution of five features of the parent participation activities to program effectiveness; and the effects of programs upon parent behavior.

The Effect of Parent Training
Programs on Child Outcomes

The evaluations of programs selected for review were internal assessments, planned and conducted by the staff of the programs themselves. This summary presents their findings at face value. We do comment, however, on features of the design or procedures that may affect the validity and generalizability of the findings. It is important to recognize that the initial purpose of these programs was to have an impact on the children involved; the evaluation effort typically was second priority. In some instances, the rigor of the evaluation design was consciously sacrificed for the benefit of the overall program or for ethical considerations. These contraints, together with the limitations imposed by field conditions of this type of research, mean that the design of the evaluations are sometimes less than ideal. The weight of the evidence from these evaluations comes from the fact that, in a general sense, they represent replications. Jamison, Suppes and Wells (1974), in their review of evaluations of educational innovations, assert that the quality of evaluation designs is uncorrelated with the results. This gives the consistency of the findings from these studies a particular significance.

In evaluating parent training programs, one feature that contributes to credibility is the nature of measures used. The staffs of the projects described in this report used ad hoc and nonreferenced assessment instruments to examine the impact of their curricular efforts, as well as standardized intelligence tests. There are obviously sound arguments for the use of specially developed tests and for criterion-referenced devices; these measures serve specific purposes for the program staff. To facilitate cross-program comparisons, however, this summary relies for the most part on instruments that are more widely known and for which some normative information is available. We recognize, of course, that the norming procedures for many "standardized" tests may be faulty, particularly with regard to the inclusion of low income and minority children, and data from the tests must be interpreted with caution.

Overall Effects of the Programs

The criteria used in evaluating the effectiveness of the programs focus on outcomes assumed to be relevant to school performance, since increased school performance is the ultimate goal of these intervention efforts. The criteria are:

o   immediate advantages on intelligence tests for program children compared with control (non-program) children;

o   long-term advantages on intelligence or achievement tests for program children compared with control children; and

o   performance in school for program children compared with control children.

The summaries of the evaluation results are grouped by (a) immediate outcomes in children's performance; (b) long-term outcomes; (c) level of school performance in both academic and social areas.

Immediate Outcomes on Intelligence Tests. Of the twenty-eight programs shown in Table 1, all but three[1] evaluated the performance of program children or program and control children on norm-referenced intelligence tests. Among the twenty-five programs using IQ tests, twenty-two produced either significant differences between program and control children or significant gains for program children by the immediate end of the intervention. In addition, the programs that used either nonstandardized measures or measures other than standardized intelligence tests also reported significant gains for program children at the end of intervention. Thus, programs that train parents as teachers of their own children are apparently successful in producing significant immediate advantages for children. The twenty-one programs that reported both pre- and post-test scores are shown in Figures 1 and 2.

_____

[1]The Structured Language Program compared program and control children but did not use a norm-referenced test. The evaluation of the Parent-Child Course used questionnaires and a criterion-referenced test; no control group was formed. The sponsors did not want to operate their program in an experimental mode, i.e., using community participants as "subjects" and forming a control group that received no treatment. The available reports on the Teaching Parents Teaching Program did not include data on children's performance.

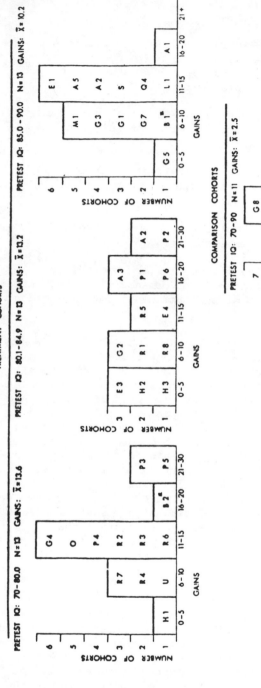

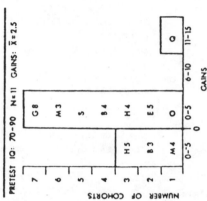

Figure 1. Mean pre-post gains by program cohorts, grouped by pretest IQ level. "Cohort" is a single treatment or comparison group within a program. Letters refer to cohorts listed in Table 1. Starred cohorts had not completed the full multiyear intervention program.

FIGURE 1 (con't).
TREATMENT COHORTS
COMPARISON COHORTS

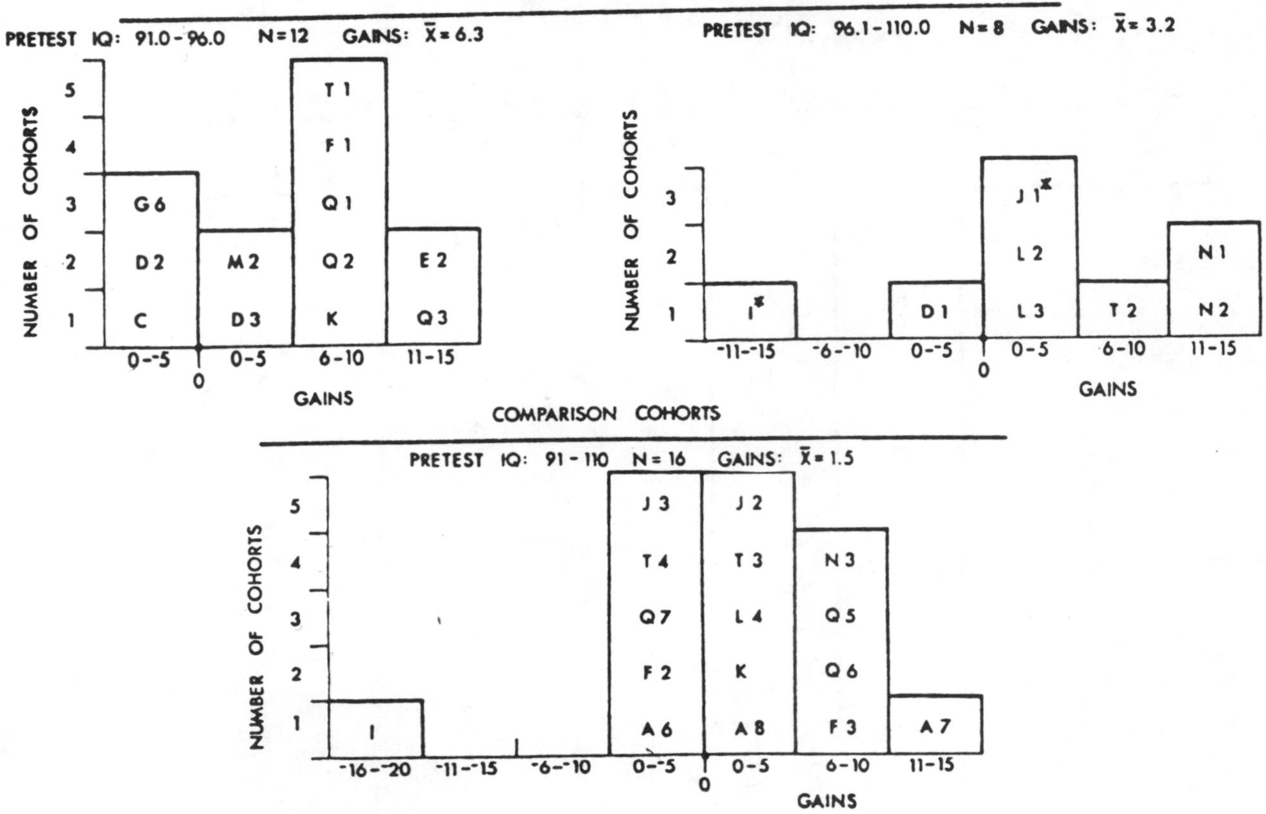

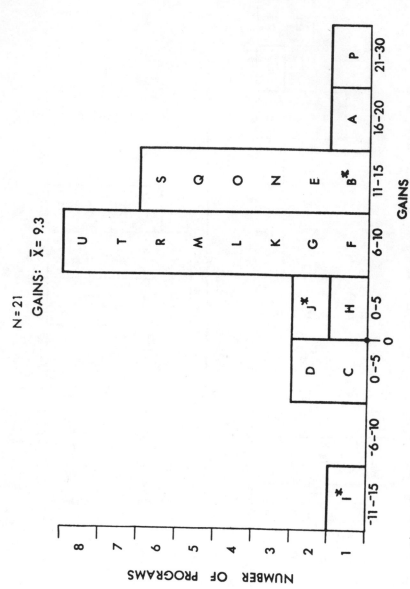

Figure 2. Mean pre-post IQ gains by programs, cohorts combined. Starred cohorts had not completed the full multi-year intervention program.

Figure 1 shows immediate pre-post test gains by program
cohort. Most of the programs included more than a single
treatment and comparison group in their evaluation design.
These "cohorts" are described briefly in Table 1. The columns
in the charts in Figure 1 list the program cohorts identified
with a given magnitude of gain. The cohorts included in
Figure 1 are grouped by the level of pretest IQ. The data
are arranged in order from lowest to highest initial IQ level.
Data for <u>programs</u> are summarized in Figure 2. The advantage
of all experimental groups over control groups is clear from
the data of Figure 1. This advantage is greatest in groups
whose initial level of IQ is relatively low, but holds for all
groups.

A methodological concern with respect to pre-post gains
in studies of intervention with low income children is the
possibility that regression to the mean accounts for the
change in mean IQ level, thus creating a false impression of
program effects. This seems not to account for gains in these
programs. The changes in IQ in control groups is near zero
regardless of initial IQ; the gains that occur are much lower
than the gains of treatment groups (Figure 1).

<u>Long-term Outcomes</u>. Follow-up testing was part of the
evaluation plan of eight programs. Four additional programs
have indicated their intention to carry out follow-up testing
in the future. As used here, "follow-up testing" refers to
assessment after the program intervention has ended. Time
lapses before (or between) follow-up testing sessions for the
programs included in this summary range from three months to
five years. In summarizing long-term results, programs are
grouped roughly into intermediate and long-range categories,
according to the time intervals between the end of the program and the first follow-up testing.

<u>Results from standardized intelligence test performance</u>.
Eight programs carried out follow-up testing of children's
intellectual performance. Seven of the eight programs
reported positive or significant differences favoring the
program children in follow-up testing over varying lengths of
time. Figure 3 shows the results obtained by the sixteen
program cohorts on IQ tests (usually the Stanford-Binet).

Two of the programs carried out follow-up testing <u>four
or more years</u> after the intervention ended. In the Ypsilanti
Perry Preschool Program, children were tested several times
up to the end of Grade III, by which time they had been out
of the program for four years. In third grade, there was not

FIGURE 3.

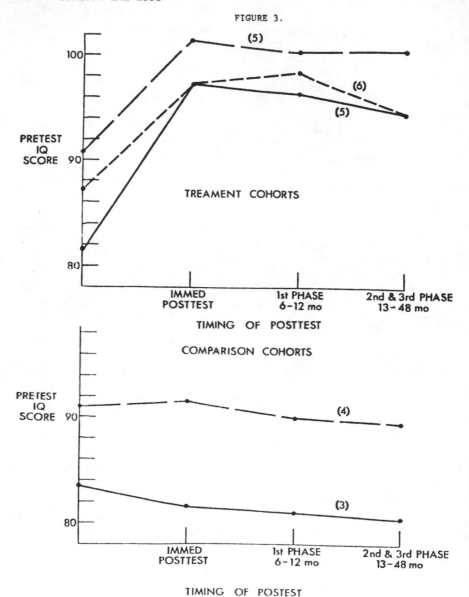

Figure 3. IQ gains by program cohorts with scores from pre- and posttest, 1st phase follow-up and 2nd or 3rd phase follow-up, grouped by pretest IQ level. Number of cohorts in each group is indicated in parentheses.

a significant difference between program and control children
in average IQ score, although there had been significant differences previous to that point. Children in the Early Training Project were followed through Grade IV, five years after
the preschool intervention had ended. There was a small but
significant difference between program and control children
at the end of fourth grade. In both the Early Training Program and the Perry Preschool Program, the between-group differences that were significant at the immediate end of intervention gradually declined after intervention ended.

Three programs carried out follow-up testing two or
three years after the end of intervention: (1) Children from
the Early Child Stimulation through Parent Education Program
were followed through first grade, three years after termination of participation in the program. At the end of Grade I,
program children remained significantly superior to control
children in average IQ score. The magnitude of the between-
group differences was similar at the end of intervention and
the end of Grade I. Children who had participated for the
full three years of the program retained nearly all of their
original ten point gain in IQ score. Children with fewer
years of participation declined in score, although all but
one group of program children scored higher than their control group. (2) In the Mother-Child Home Program children
were followed through first grade. Children who received the
full two years of intervention have maintained nearly 100% of
the large gains shown in immediate posttesting. The difference in average IQ between the program and control children
at the end of Grade I was significant and similar in magnitude to the difference at the end of the intervention. (3)
Two years after their program participation ended, children
in the Learning to Learn Program were in third grade. During the two years after the program, the difference in average IQ for program and control children remained large and
significant. Both groups, however, declined slightly but
consistently in IQ through second and third grades.

For three programs, follow-up data were obtained on children one year after intervention ended. (1) In the Ypsilanti-
Carnegie Infant Education Project, follow-up after one year
showed no significant difference between program and control
children, although program children did have a higher average score. Both groups scored above the national average.
(2) One year after their participation in the Ypsilanti
Early Education Program children who had attended the preschool classes and whose parents had participated in classes
and home visits continued to gain in IQ score (on the Peabody Picture Vocabulary Test) and scored higher than children
who had received preschool classes only. This same trend was

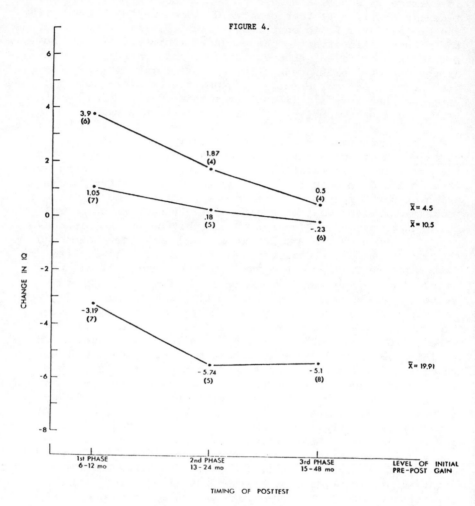

Figure 4. Follow-up changes in IQ level of program cohorts, grouped by level of initial gain. Total number of cohorts in each group and number of cohorts for each data point is indicated in parentheses.

not confirmed on the Wechsler Intelligence Scale for Children. (3) The Birmingham Parent-Child Development Center obtained test scores from four-year-old children who had been in the program for one year only and for whom one year had elapsed since the end of the intervention. Program children had a significantly higher average IQ score than control children. The between-group difference in IQ appeared to increase with time: That is, program children were increasing in average IQ score, while control children were decreasing.

As a group, parent training programs gave children at termination of intervention an advantage over control children in average IQ score. In the programs that carried out follow-up testing, the advantage was sustained into grade school. In about one-half of the programs that assessed long-term performance, however, there was a gradual decrease in IQ score from a high score at the immediate end of the intervention. This decline was usually much less than the initial gains (Figure 3). Both program and control children declined the score; program children usually continue to score higher. The decline was similar in magnitude across level of pretest IQ.

Figure 4 shows post treatment changes in IQ points for cohorts with three different levels of initial pre-post gains (4.5; 10.5; 19.9). The group of cohorts with the lowest average gain at program end were still slightly above their posttest score at the third pause of follow-up. The cohorts who showed the greatest gain at posttest suffered some loss in follow-up (about 5 IQ points); this decline was only about one-fourth of the magnitude of the initial gains.

Results from achievement test performance. Three program evaluations included school grades or performance on standardized achievement tests. These were the Ypsilanti Perry Preschool Program, the Learning to Learn Program, and the Early Training Project. All three showed positive results.

The Ypsilanti Perry Preschool Program reported data on achievement test scores for children through the fourth grade. On the California Achievement Test, program children scored higher than control children at each year's posttesting, although the difference was significantly only through third grade. In third grade, none of the control children scored above the 50th percentile on the test, while half the program children did. Also, 72% of the program children were at their expected grade level by third grade, compared with only

60% of control children. Substantially more control children
had been assigned to special remedial classes. These differences in performance were evident even though the scores
on standardized IQ tests in third grade did not show a significant difference favoring program children.

In the Early Training Project, program children significantly out-scored control children on a standardized achievement test through second grade. By fourth grade, the difference remained but was no longer significant.

School grades of children from the Learning to Learn
Program were compared with the grades of control children.
At the end of third grade, 92% of the program children were
receiving passing grades while only 60% of control children
were. Twenty-six percent of program children were at or
above their expected grade level, compared with 8% for the
control group. Only 3% of the program children had fallen
more than a year and one-half below grade level, compared
with 32% of control children. Children in the program were
consistently superior to children in the control group in
grades in reading, arithmetic, and language ability. On
achievement tests in reading, arithmetic, and language, more
than half the program children scored at or above their
expected level; less than 20% of control children did so.

Few of the evaluations included evidence of long-term
differences between program and control children in academic
achievement. Where evidence was obtained, it showed an advantage for children with the special preschool experience. Two
effects showed up consistently: Program children were more
likely to maintain performance at grade level and were less
likely to require special classes. These benefits are obviously central to the evaluation of impact where the ultimate
goal is to affect performance in school. The data from the
Ypsilanti Perry Preschool Program suggest that, even where
IQ differences between control and program children become
insignificant, there may continue to be a significant impact
upon school performance.

Results from measures of school social behavior. Three
evaluations included teachers' assessment of children's classroom behavior. All three showed that children who had
received preschool intervention had an advantage over the
nonprogram children. For the children from the Ypsilanti
Perry Preschool Program, socioemotional ratings by teachers
in Grades I and II significantly favored program children.
By Grade III, the program children were rated higher but not
significantly so. At each age of follow-up testing, children

from the Mother-Child Home Program were given above average ratings by teachers on their school psychosocial behavior. Ratings for program children were consistently higher than those for control children. In the Learning to Learn Program, teacher ratings favored program children: 70% compared with 53% of control children were rated as having an "appropriate" self-concept. On ratings of achievement motivation, all program children from the Learning to Learn Program were placed above the minimum level considered necessary for school success, while only 8% of the control children received at least the minimum rating.

Conclusions. These intervention programs were success-ful in providing children with both immediate and long-term advantages in skills that are relevant to school performance. These are represented in initial gains in IQ scores, which, although they decline a bit, still show gains maintained over the length of time spanned by these evaluations. The results from achievement tests, grades, and grade placement were highly consistent in displaying evidence of gains from the program. Although not of central concern, teacher ratings of children's social adjustment also consistently distinguished between program and control children.

Differential Effects of the Programs on Children's IQ Scores

Five features of the parent participation were identi-fied as potentially important to program effectiveness. These were

(1) importance of the instruction-to-parents phase in the total program;

(2) curricular focus of the parent teaching activi-ties;

(3) teacher/parent ratio in instruction-to-parents;

(4) degree of structure in the parent teaching activities; and

(5) degree of specificity in the instruction-to-parents.

Differences among the programs in immediate and long-term effectiveness were examined in relation to program vari-ation on the five features. In investigating the effects of these features, we grouped the programs into levels (e.g., "high," "medium," and "low") on each.

Table 2

Predictors of Program Effectiveness

Program Title	Program Format	Content of Parent Component	Teacher/ Parent Ratio	Structure/ Specificity of Parent Component
Mother-Child Home Program (Levenstein)	Home visits	Verbal[1]	1 – 1	High/High
Houston Parent-Child Development Center (Lelar)	Year 1: Home visits Year 2: Parent classes, pre-school	Cognitive	1 – 1	High/Med
		Cognitive	1-group	Med/Med
First Generation Mother Study (Barbrack)	Home visits	Cognitive	1 – 1	Med/Med
Infant Intervention Project (Forrester)	Home visits	Cognitive	1 – 1	Med/Med
Second Generation Mother Study (Barbrack)	Home visits	Cognitive	1 – 1	Med/Med
Study of Intrafamily Effects (Gilmer & Gray)	Home visits	Cognitive	1 – 1	Med/Med
Ypsilanti-Carnegie Infant Education Project (Lambie, Weikart, Bond)	Home visits	Cognitive	1 – 1	Med/Med

Table 2 continued

Program Title	Program Format	Content of Parent Component	Teacher/ Parent Ratio	Structure/ Specificity of Parent Component
Early Child Stimulation Through Parent Education Program (Gordon)	Home visits	Sensory-motor	1 – 1	High/Med
Three Home Visiting Strategies (Barbrack)	Home visits	Cognitive Sens-motor	1 – 1	Med/Med
Birmingham Parent-Child Development Center (Lasater, Malone)	Preschool classes for both mother & child together	Cognitive	1-group (1-1)[2]	Med/Med
New Orleans Parent-Child Development Center (Andrews, Bache)	Preschool classes for both mother & child together or home visits	Cognitive Child Devel.	1-group (1-1)	Med/Med
Parent-Child Course (Rayder)	Parent classes	Cognitive	1-group	High/High
Mothers Training Program (Karnes)	Parent classes	Cognitive (Verbal)	1-group (1-1)	High/Med
Home-Oriented Preschool Education (Appalachian Educational Laboratory)	Home visits TV programs preschool	Cognitive	1 – 1	Med/Med

Table 2 continued

Program Title	Program Format	Content of Parent Component	Teacher/ Parent Ratio	Structure/ Specificity of Parent Component
Early Training Project (Gray & Klaus)	Home visits preschool	Cognitive	1 – 1	Med/Med
Special Kindergarten Intervention Program (Radin)	Home visits preschool	Cognitive	1 – 1	Med/Med
Ypsilanti Perry Preschool Program (Weikart)	Home visits preschool	Cognitive (Verbal)	1 – 1	Med/Med
Ypsilanti Curriculum Demonstration Project	Home visits preschool	Cognitive	1 – 1	Med/Med
Spanish Dame Bilingual Education Program (Micotti)	Home visits preschool with parent present	Cognitive Verbal	1 – 1	Med/Med
Ypsilanti Early Education Program (Kingston & Radin)	Home visits parent classes preschool	Cognitive	1 – 1 1-group	Med/Med
Hawaii Program I (Adkins)	Parent classes parent aides preschool	Cognitive	1-group (1-1)	Med/Med
Hawaii Program II (Adkins)	Parent classes parent aides preschool	Cognitive Child Devel.	1-group (1-1)	Med/Med

Table 2 continued

Program Title	Program Format	Content of Parent Component	Teacher/Parent Ratio	Structure/Specificity of Parent Component
Hawaii Program III (Adkins)	Parent classes parent aides preschool	Cognitive	1-group (1-1)	Med/Med
Learning to Learn Program (Sprigle)	Parent classes conferences preschool	Cognitive Child Devel.	1-group (1-1)	Med/Med
Structured Language Program (Mann)	Parent classes preschool	Verbal	1-group (1-)	Med/High
Teaching Parents Teaching (Champagne & Goldman)	Parent classes preschool	Verbal	1-group (1-1)	Med/High
Parents are Teachers Too Program (Boger)	Parent classes preschool	1st: Verbal 2nd: Sensory-motor	1-group	High/High
Project Early Push (Downey)	Parent classes conf., preschool	Cognitive	1-group (1-1)	Med/Med
Oakland Preschool Program (Waters)	Parent visits preschool	Child Devel.	(1-1)	Low/Low

[1]Ratings do not imply exclusive emphasis but rather dominant emphasis in a program.

[2]"(1-1)" refers to infrequent one-to-one parent/teacher meetings that are not the dominant mode in the program.

This grouping involved assumptions of similarity among programs that are not entirely justified. First, the grouping was based on descriptions provided by sponsors rather than on observations. The specific features under consideration may not be comparable across programs. Second, even where there is comparability, the total programs may differ from one another in other respects. Obviously we must be cautious. On the other hand, these programs are treatments that share characteristics such as staff enthusiasm and commitment, a high level of program planning, and the interest stimulated by a new program.

Emphasis on instruction-to-parents. Is the amount of emphasis on the instruction-to-parents related to program effectiveness? Emphasis is here defined as the proportion of program efforts allocated to instructing parents, ranging from total concentration on parents to instruction for parents that is secondary to preschool classes for the children. The twenty-eight programs were divided into two groups, thirteen programs (Set I) were judged to have "high" emphasis on the parent teaching component. Program formats in Set I included:

Home visits to parent/child pairs   (N=9)

Classes for parents   (N=2)

Classes for parent/child pairs   (N=2)

Fifteen programs (Set II) are judged to have "medium" emphasis. These programs offered either:

Preschool classes for children supplemented
by home visits to parent/child pairs or,   (N=7)

Preschool classes for children supplemented
by classes for parents   (N=8)

A comparison of the immediate effectiveness of Set I and Set II programs shows that neither group has a consistent advantage. There does appear, however, to be one aspect of program format cutting across Set I and II that is related to level of effectiveness. Home visits, either alone or in combination with preschool classes for the children, apparently are associated with higher immediate gains.

The nine programs using home visits only produced gains ranging from 0 to 18 IQ points, with an average level of gains around 8 points. The programs that combined home visits

with preschool classes showed gains ranging from 9 to 15
points, with an average around 10 points. The remaining
twelve programs produced an average gain of around 6 IQ
points.

Eight programs reported data from follow-up testing.
Four fall in Set I; four in Set II. In Set I, three of the
four programs reported that children's immediate gains were
maintained in follow-up. In the fourth program, program
children were superior to control children in follow-up, although there was a decline in scores for both groups.

All four of the Set II programs with follow-up results
reported that program children maintained an advantage over
control children, although both groups declined.

Set I programs produced more durable long-term gains,
although the programs in both sets reported positive effects
for program children in follow-up. There is one caution in
this conclusion: The eight programs are compared regardless
of the length of time covered in follow-up testing, and Set
II programs involved longer follow-up periods. Since it
appears that erosion of gains frequently begins in middle
elementary grades, the Set II programs may appear less effective because of the timing of follow-up testing.

Curricular Focus of the Parent Teaching Activities. Is
the curricular focus of the parent teaching activities related to program effectiveness? The programs were divided into
three groups:

Programs with parent activities focused on
children's verbal development   (N=5)

Programs with parent activities focused on
children's sensory-motor development   (N=3)

Programs with parent activities focused on
children's general cognitive development   (N=20)

None of these three categories is clearly related to
program effectiveness, either immediate or long-term. This
conclusion is not a surprise, in the light of previous comparisons of curricula in compensatory education (Weikart,
1969).

In three programs, the comparison groups were formed so
as to investigate the effectiveness of different curricular
components. In the Early Child Stimulation through Parent
Education Program, two curricula for home visits were com-

pared. One consisted of tasks based on Piagetian theory;
the other consisted of tasks developed by the paraprofessional Parent Educators. No significant differences were
found between the performance of children receiving the two
curricula. In Barbrack's study of Three Home Visiting
Strategies, training based on sensory-motor tasks was compared with training based on tasks aimed at cognitive stimulation. There was no significant difference in magnitude of
immediate IQ gains made by the children of the two groups of
mothers. Barbrack concluded that curricula taken equally
seriously by mothers would have similar effects on the children. On the other hand, mothers in the cognitively based
group made greater positive changes in their teaching behavior than did the mothers in the sensory-motor group. In the
University of Hawaii Program II, two curricula for parents
were compared; one curriculum emphasized child development
principles, and the other emphasized the parents' role in the
child's cognitive development. Parent participation in the
cognitive development program benefited the children (i.e.,
increased their gains), while parent participation in the
child development program did little to facilitate the children's progress.

On the one hand, it can be cautiously concluded that no
one content for parent programs (as described in program
materials) consistently produced higher or more stable gains
for program children. On the other hand, this statement by
itself is incomplete. Certain factors in parent programs other
than content seem to make a difference. An example is the
validity of the curriculum in the parent's eyes. Further, it
seems that the content of a curriculum may be less important
in determining program effectiveness than how the curriculum
involves parents. In the University of Hawaii program, the
more effective curriculum emphasized parents' responsibility
in their child's development, which may have made a difference
in the extent or quality of the parents' participation.

Teacher/parent ratio. Is program effectiveness related
to the ratio of teachers to parents in the instruction-to-
parent activities? Is it more effective to work with parents individually in a one-to-one relationship, or as a class
in a one-to-group relationship? Both kinds of program organization offer advantages. One-to-one interaction, usually in
home visits, offers the possibility of a more intense parent/
teacher relationship and greater potential for personal rap-
port; group classes offer the possibility of support and
motivation among group members.

In a first attempt to answer the question, the nine programs that used home visits only (one-to-one ratio) were

compared with the four programs with parent classes only
(one-to-group). The home visit programs produced high immediate gains more often than the program with parent classes;
the home visit programs also showed long-term maintenance
of gains in follow-up. The apparent superiority of the home
visit programs is a tentative finding, however. We lack data
on the four "parent classes" programs; only two of the programs reported comparable immediate test scores and only one
program carried out follow-up testing.

A second assessment of one-to-one vs. one-to-group
teacher/parent relationships compares programs that combine
preschool classes and home visits with programs that combine
preschool classes and parent classes. There are seven of the
former and ten of the latter type. Average level of immediate IQ gain appears to be slightly but consistently higher
for the "preschool plus home visits" programs. Long-term
results could not be used, since only one "preschool plus
parent classes" program reported data. The apparent advantage of the "preschool plus home visit" programs in this
comparison supports the conclusion that home visits are an
effective format.

Structure in the parent teaching activities. Is degree
of structure in the parent teaching activities related to
program effectiveness? "High structure" is defined as a
program that develops a sequence of predetermined concrete
tasks for parents. Seven programs were rated as "high" in
structure; the rest were judged to have "medium" structure.

Degree of structure was not clearly related to level of
immediate IQ gains, although it is true that the programs
with a high degree of structure consistently produced at
least moderate short-term gains. Degree of structure does
appear to be related to long-term program effectiveness, in
terms of stability of gains. The two programs with the best
follow-up records were "high" structure programs.

Programs with high structure offer parents concrete
activities. These may serve parents as clear guides for working with their children. Concrete tasks may motivate parents
to practice new behaviors with their child by offering unam-
biguous instructions and activities. In terms of long-term
benefits, parents who develop a repertoire of specific activities may be more likely to carry out such activities in the
future, since the tasks become part of their competence --
understandable and practiced. Continuing parent/child interaction around these tasks might be one reason for the maintenance of gains by program children in the highly structured
programs. On the other hand, less structure in a parent com-

ponent can mean that the tasks are individualized for each
parent, as in the Ypsilanti Infant Education Project. There
may be special advantages for less structured parent components, if less structure implies individual prescription of
tasks.

Specificity in instruction-to-parents. The level of
specificity in parent instruction is defined as the degree of
definition or detail: Are parents trained to use specific
teaching techniques or is a general style of interaction
encouraged?

Six programs were judged "high" in specificity. The
rest were judged to have "moderate" specificity. Level of
specificity is not systematically related to greater program
effectiveness, either immediate or long-term.

Within-program comparisons of the effects of parent
training. The designs of a small number of programs permit-
ted more controlled comparisons of intervention with and without instruction-to-parents. HOPE (Home Oriented Preschool
Education) program sponsors compared the effects of three
program components: televised lessons for children, home
visits to teach children and their parents, and small group
classes for children in a mobile classroom. Home visits appeared to be most strongly associated with the children's
cognitive and language development, and this component was
the only one in which parents participated. The evaluation
of SKIP (Special Kindergarten Intervention Program) separated
the effects of the children's supplementary classroom component, their normal kindergarten experience, and a parent
involvement component. The involvement was one-to-one advis-
ing of mothers by a home visitor, concentrating on changing
the mothers' teaching. The highest scores for program children at the immediate end of the program was for group with
parent involvement.

In two studies, the effect of parent participation was
investigated by relating an indicator of involvement -- attendance at parent activities -- to the magnitude of children's
immediate IQ gains. In both Project Early Push and the programs from the University of Hawaii, children of parents who
participated more often in the parent activities outscored
children whose parents were less involved or uninvolved. The
conclusion common to these programs was that greater parent
involvement was related to higher gains.

Conclusions. The twenty-eight programs were consistently successful in producing immediate gains on standardized
intelligence tests and lasting advantages in test scores for

program children. The consistent effectiveness of these programs suggests that parent training is important to program
success. This is supported by the data from the few programs
that compared treatments with and without parent training.

The five major features of the program are only modest-
ly related to magnitude of program effectiveness. They do
not account for the very large differences among effects of
different programs. Some relationships do appear, however,
and may be summarized as follows:

1. Importance of the instruction-to-parents. Data
from immediate testing favored home visits, either alone or
in combination with preschool classes for the children. The
long-term data also indicated greater effectiveness for programs with emphasis on parents. Assuming that the programs
identified as having greater emphasis on parents did so
in practice, then it appears that the more a program is focused on the parents, the more likely it is to produce significant and stable IQ gains for children. This trend in the
cross-program comparisons is consistent with the conclusion
from the within-program comparisons.

2. Curricular focus of the parent teaching activities.
No single curriculum of parent teaching activities was favored by the outcome criteria. Although program content that
requires the active involvement of parents appears likely to
produce higher gains for children, such change seems to follow from curricular format rather than content.

3. Teacher/parent ratio in instruction-to-parents.
Greater effects in immediate and follow-up testing are produced by a one-to-one parent/teacher relationship.

4. Degree of structure in the parent teaching activities. High structure (the use of predetermined concrete
tasks) in parent training is related to higher program effectiveness.

5. Degree of specificity in the instruction-to-parents.
There was no relationship between level of specificity in
parent instruction and program effectiveness.

The trends from the cross-program comparisons seem consistent in underlining the importance of active involvement
of parents in preschool programs.

The Effectiveness of Parent Training
Programs on Parents

Overall Effects of the Programs

Although the primary interest of evaluation studies of
these programs was in child outcomes, about half of the
twenty-eight project staffs also assessed the impact upon
parents. The results are even more difficult to compare
across programs than are assessments of child outcomes, since
there are no standardized and few widely used instruments
for measuring changes in parents that might be expected as a
result of participation. A summary of program effects upon
parents must be based on results from instruments for which
information on norms, reliability and validity is not available. Such experimental instruments, however, do permit
comparisons within programs between participating parents
and parents in control groups.

Even though a variety of instruments were used in these
evaluations, there are major areas of parent behavior that
were commonly examined in the evaluations: Parent attitudes,
parent/child interactions, and home environments. It was in
these areas that changes were expected.

Outcome data for parents are available only for immediate posttesting; so far, follow-up data have not been
reported, although they are being collected in some programs.
Such follow-up data on parents are obviously important to
indicate whether the programs create a relatively permanent
change in the child's home environment and thus offer continuing impact upon the program children and upon other children in the family. Perhaps most crucial, evidence of effects upon parents addresses the question of whether or not
the impact of programs upon children come from the contact of
the child with his parent or from contact with the home visitor or other staff members. If parents display no new behavior or attitudes, it is difficult to dismiss the alternate
hypothesis that the program staff has a direct influence on
the child.

Immediate outcomes in parent attitudes. The two parental attitudes for which significant changes were most often
found were (1) sense of personal efficacy or control over
one's own life, and (2) attitude toward one's child and his/
her development.

In three programs, Early Child Stimulation through
Parent Education Program, Program II from Hawaii Center for
Research in Early Childhood Education, and New Orleans
Parent-Child Development Center, mothers who participated in

the training significantly increased their sense of personal efficacy compared to their pretest level, or scored significantly higher than control mothers. In the Hawaii Program, the more active parents were in the training, the greater was their sense of personal efficacy by the end of the program. Change in parents' sense of internal control appeared in data from a variety of instruments.

Program sponsors also expected parents to acquire more realistic and flexible expectations about their child's development. Evaluation of four programs found evidence that mothers became more flexible during the intervention. The Ypsilanti Early Education Project and the Birmingham Parent-Child Development Center used the Parent Attitude Research Instrument (PARI). Mothers in the Ypsilanti program decreased on the Authoritatianism subscale, and the amount of change was related to the intensity of the mother's participation. Mothers in the Birmingham program made greater positive changes than control mothers in ten of the PARI subscales. The Birmingham Parent-Child Development Center and the Houston Parent-Child Development Center found evidence of changing developmental expectations of their children on different measures. The Ypsilanti-Carnegie Infant Education Project did <u>not</u> find that the program altered the parents' developmental expectation of their child.

Of the six programs that assessed change in parent attitudes, five found positive evidence, although the results were not always statistically significant. There was a consistency across programs and instruments in the attitudes most often found to have changed -- sense of personal power, authoritarian attitudes toward one's own child, and developmental expectations.

Changes in these attitudes conceivably could contribute to gains in child performance, assuming that they represent shifts in parent behavior. The possibility of a relationship between changes in parental attitudes and gains in children's performance was examined in only one study (Gordon and Jester, 1972) and no relationship was found. This is obviously not a basis for conclusions about these studies.

<u>Immediate Outcomes in Parent/Child Interactions</u>. Parent training programs apparently affect the pattern of interaction between parents and children. Evaluation designs which included assessment of changes in parent-child interaction found significant program effects in both parents' verbal and nonverbal behavior (e.g., teaching style or level of responsiveness).

Verbal behavior. Several different instruments (often experimental) were used to assess parents' language during interactions with their child. The results consistently showed evidence of change in parents' patterns of language in the desired directions. The two aspects of parents' verbal behavior that were most commonly assessed were (a) use of language to reinforce or support the child's efforts, and (b) use of syntactically complex or varied language patterns.

In three programs the effect of the intervention upon frequency of use of supportive language was assessed. In all three (Ypsilanti Infant Education Project, Teaching Parents Teaching, and Second Generation Mother Study) program mothers significantly increased their use of verbal reinforcement or positive feedback while teaching their children. In the latter two studies, program mothers also decreased their use of negative feedback.

In three programs (Structured Language, Parents Are Teachers Too, New Orleans Parent-Child Development Center) some aspect of the syntax of parental language -- variety of sentence types, specificity of language, syntactic complexity -- was assessed. The Structured Language Program trained mothers in specific new language patterns. These mothers, by the end of the program, used a more advanced syntax and a greater range of language interaction patterns than did controls. In the Parents Are Teachers Too Program, parents in language intervention groups began to use more specific language to help their child on tasks. In the New Orleans Parent-Child Development Center, the language of program mothers became more elaborated, and the mothers more often expanded on their child's verbalizations and elicited verbal responses from their child.

In six programs, parents' language behavior was assessed in parent/child teaching situations. Positive change was found in each on at least one aspect of language. Most of the measures used included several subscales, and, typically, change was found on only some of these subscales.

Nonverbal behavior. A variety of nonverbal behaviors during parent/child interaction was also assessed. The instruments typically used were experimental observation techniques.

One major aspect of nonverbal behavior studies was the social responsiveness of the parent to the child. In three programs (the Ypsilanti Infant Education Project, the Houston Parent-Child Development Center, and the Birmingham Parent-Child Development Center), parents were judged to be more responsive, warmer, more sensitive, or more relaxed with their

children when compared with control parent/child pairs at the
end of or during intervention.

A second aspect of nonverbal behavior studied was degree
of active participation by parents during interactions with
their child or during teaching tasks. In the Barbrack study
of home visiting strategies and the New Orleans Parent-Child
Development Center, program parents were rated as participating more actively than control parents during interaction
with their children.

In all five programs in which parents' nonverbal behavior
was examined, significant differences between program and control parents were observed. The consistently positive results
in these two major areas suggest that these intervention programs did change parents' nonverbal behaviors with their children in ways hypothesized to stimulate the child's development.

Immediate Changes in the Home Environment. In these
evaluations, the impact of programs upon two aspects of home
environments were examined: changes in the performance of
siblings and changes in the quality of the stimulation in the
home.

Changes in siblings in program families. Program sponsors hypothesized that parents who received training as
teachers of their own child would use their new skills with
both the "target" child in the program and with other children. Improvement in sibling performance over the period of
the intervention, therefore, could be seen as an indication
that program parents were changing their home behavior. Siblings in program families were tested in the Early Training
Project and the Study of Intrafamily Diffusion Effects. Both
studies found that the younger siblings in families where
parents participated in some kind of training scored significantly higher than control children on a standardized IQ
test. The results supported the hypothesis that intervention
produced changes in the parents' home behaviors which benefited the intellectual development of all the children in the
home.

Changes in the stimulation in the home. Staffs of five
programs evaluated changes in the home environments of program and control families, using the Cognitive Home Environment Scale or Caldwell's Home Inventory. Three programs --
The Ypsilanti Early Education Program, Special Kindergarten
Intervention Program, and Early Child Stimulation through
Parent Education Program -- found that program families
clearly scored higher on the home measures than did control
families or families who had received treatments that were

not focused on training them as teachers. In the Early Child
Stimulation through Parent Education Program, the differences
were found at the one-year follow-up testing. In the Houston
Parent-Child Development Center, first-year results did not
clearly favor program parents. After families had been in
the program for two years, a trend emerged favoring program
over control families on measure of home environment. In
the Ypsilanti Perry Preschool Program, no significant differences were found between the groups of families at the end
of intervention.

Other Changes in Parents. Some of the program evaluations reported an increase in parent initiative in gaining
new skills or new positions in the community. The Birmingham
Parent-Child Development Center, Project Early Push, and the
Study of Intrafamily Diffusion Effects all reported that
program parents made important changes in their lives in the
direction of greater self-sufficiency and effectiveness.

Differential Effects of the
Programs on Parents

The data available were not sufficiently comparable to
provide a basis for conclusions about whether some programs
are more effective than others in producing changes in parents. Also, since the programs that did examine parent behavior were relatively similar in the features of their parent training, we could not compare different program features.

Discussion

The programs summarized here consistently produced significant immediate gains in children's IQ scores, which
seemed to be maintained in about half of the programs that
carried out follow-up testing. They also appeared to affect
school performance in a positive direction and influence the
language, attitudes, and teaching behavior of parents. The
success of these parent training programs suggest that parent participation of this type is an important component of
early intervention programs.

Although almost all of the programs were successful in
producing gains in children, some were apparently more effective than others. The reasons for this differential effectiveness were not clearly identified. The features of parent participation that were hypothesized to be related to
program effectiveness are not strongly associated with outcomes, although some are related at a modest level. In general, however, these features are not adequate to explain
differences in success among programs.

Descriptions of programs provided us by the sponsors indicate that the programs were designed to be quite different from one another in approach, curriculum, and procedures. These sponsor-defined differences, however, were not systematically related to variation in outcome. Since programs were not observed as part of the procedures for this review, there may be a discrepancy between the written description of activities and their implementation. However, recent observational records of classroom implementations of early education curricula show that the classroom activities often closely match the sponsors' descriptions of program design (Stallings, 1976). Even so, attempts to relate program features to outcomes yielded only incomplete data.

The lack of evidence for clearly different effects of presumably distinct treatment variables might be thought to suggest that the interprogram variation is random. This seems unlikely, however, for two reasons. First, programs that replicated their treatment usually found consistent results; second, there is little overlap among programs in the magnitude of gains produced in multiple replications.

If such variation among programs is not randomly distributed, the sources are unidentified. Whatever these may be, they are themselves not randomly distributed across programs. They may, thus, be associated in some way with the character of the total program approach. What does appear to be emerging in these and other data (Weikart, 1969; Miller & Dyer, 1976) is that it is easier to produce effects in intervention programs than it is to identify the specific factors which contribute to success. On the basis of our data we would suggest that it is not the curriculum but the mode of dealing with the mothers, particularly the degree of specificity in the instruction-to-parents, that is associated with gain.

It is possible that the immediate effect of these programs is caused by factors unrelated to the specific treatments. All of the programs provided social reinforcement in the form of increased attention paid by the staff to the families involved. All projects were experimental and thus new, with a relatively enthusiastic, committed staff, new equipment, funds, and other signs of an exciting and promising venture. Some of these conditions may have created a Hawthorne effect in the program staff, and possibly in the families, which may be an effective feature common to these programs. The potential effects of nonexperimental factors, such as social reinforcement from the staff and from school personnel, are confounded with the treatment effects in most of the evaluation designs. The two-group, experimental vs. control design, usually does not separate the two types of effects.   The impact of the programs may accrue from these nonexperimental factors.

A final comment about these programs concerns the ethics of intervention.   In the appreciation of the apparent suc- cess of these programs, we might, as professionals, consider the role that we have played and the involvement of the fam- ilies with whom we work.   Families were not involved in the decisions which led to the program design and implementation. Program sponsors made most of the decisions -- they saw the need, planned, initiated, and administered the programs.   The families made the decision whether or not to participate.

These programs usually are designed by middle class pro- fessionals; the parent components are relatively didactic; the content of the training is determined by professionals; and the goals for training -- the "optimal" parenting style -- are established by the program sponsors.   The programs bring a standard of parenting into the lives of low income families that is modeled to some degree on the middle class family ideal type.   This is especially true of the programs started several years ago; those developed more recently have moved away somewhat from predominantly professional control to include parents' ideas in planning and parents' own goals.

Parents share the desire to have their children achieve at a satisfactory level in schools.   These programs thus bring together the middle class professional and the low income families at a point of common values and aspirations. Perhaps these programs eventually will combine in a more reciprocal way the right of parents to decide the character of their own experience and their child's education and the technical resources that professionals can bring to bear on the development of specific educational skills.

References

Bloom, B. S. <u>Stability and change in human characteristics</u>. New York: John Wiley & Sons, Inc., 1964.

Brim, O. G. <u>Education for child rearing</u>. New York: Russell Sage Foundation, 1959.

Coleman, J. S., et al. <u>Equality of educational opportunity</u>. Washington, D.C.: U.S. Office of Education, 1966.

Davis, Mary D. Nursery-Kindergarten-Primary Education in 1924-26. Washington, D.C., 1927. U.S. Bureau of Education, Bulletin No. 28.

Goodson, B. D. and Hess, R. Parents as teachers of young children: An evaluative review of some contemporary concepts and programs. Stanford, Ca.: School of Education, Stanford University, 1975.

Gordon, I. Developing parent power. In Grothberg, E. (ed.), <u>Critical issues in research related to disadvantaged children</u>. Princeton, N.J.: Educational Testing Service, 1969.

Gordon, I., and Jester, R. Instructional strategies in infant stimulation. JSAS, <u>Catalog of Selected Documents in Psychology</u>, 1972, <u>2</u>, 122.

Hess, R. D. Parental behavior and children's school achievement, implications for Head Start. In <u>Critical issues in research related to disadvantaged children</u>. Princeton, N.J.: Educational Testing Service, 1969.

Hunt, J. M. The psychological basis for using preschool enrichment as an antidote for cultural deprivation. In J. Hellmuth (ed.), <u>Disadvantaged child</u>, Vol. 1. Seattle: Special Child Publications of the Seattle Seguin School, Inc., 1967, 255-299.

Jamison, D., Suppes, P., & Wells, S. The effectiveness of alternative instructional media: A survey. <u>Review of Educational Research</u>, 1974, <u>44</u>(1), 1-69.

Jencks, C., et al. <u>Inequality: A re-assessment of the effect of family and schooling in America</u>. New York: Basic Books, 1972.

Miller, L., & Dyer, J. Four preschool programs: Their dimensions and effects. Monographs of the Society for Research in Child Development, <u>162</u>, 1975.

Schlossman, S. Before Home Start: Notes toward a history of
    parent education in America, 1897-1929. Harvard Educa-
    tional Review, July, 1976. In press.

Stallings, J. Implementation and child effects of teaching
    practices in follow through classrooms. Monographs of
    the Society for Research in Child Development, 163, 1975.

Sunley, R. Early 19th century American literature on child
    rearing. In M. Mead & M. Wolfenster (eds.), Childhood
    in contemporary culture. Chicago: University of
    Chicago Press, 1955.

Twenty-Eighth Yearbook of the National Society of the Study
    of Education. Preschool and Parental Education.
    Bloomington, Ill.: Public School Publishing Co., 1929.

Weikart, D. Ypsilanti Preschool Curriculum demonstration
    project, 1968-1971. Ypsilanti, Mich.:   High/Scope
    Educational Research Foundation, 1969.

3

Long-Term Effects of
Early Intervention
The New Haven Project

Victoria Seitz, Nancy H. Apfel and Carole Efron

One of the most difficult issues for those who must
make social policy decisions concerning special intervention
programs is whether programs such as Head Start and Follow
Through do or do not produce lasting measurable benefits.
As the authors of one review of the research on early intervention have noted, "The final question must eventually be
asked: Can children be brought to a productive level of
functioning by (intervention) programs? If the answer is
yes, we keep on doing what we are doing. If the answer is
no, the social and educational implications are enormous"
(Horowitz & Paden, 1973, p. 385).

Perhaps the single most important reason that long-
term effects are not presently well understood has been the
simple absence of empirical data. Although there have been
many studies of young children while they are enrolled in
intervention programs, there have been relatively few
studies to determine what becomes of these children after
the termination of intervention. In the case of the Head
Start program, in particular, the present authors know of
no published study examining long-term effects into adolescence. There have also been few longitudinal studies of
children receiving intervention. An earlier and much
publicized study of long-term effects, the Ohio University-
Westinghouse Report, concluded that by the end of the second
grade any gains due to the Head Start experience have disappeared and experimental and control children are performing in a manner indistinguishable from each other and un-
distinguished in comparison with national norms. Despite
its widely publicized results, however, the Westinghouse
Report, as a one-time, cross-sectional study with several
serious sampling problems (Campbell & Erlebacher, 1970;
Smith & Bissell, 1970) cannot be considered an adequate
basis for concluding that Head Start has no long-term
effects. As Ryan (1974) suggests, longitudinal information

is easier to interpret in providing evidence on this matter.

Some encouraging longitudinal data on the effects of Head Start do presently exist to suggest that children who received Head Start continue to maintain an advantage over control children on measures of IQ (Abelson, Zigler, & De Blasi, 1974) and on academic achievement (Abelson, Zigler, & DeBlasi, 1974; Stanford Research Institute, 1971a, 1971b) if they subsequently receive a continued intervention program which is similar to the Head Start program. In the studies cited, the continuation program was provided by a special "Follow Through" project. One purpose of the present study was to continue to examine the children from the Abelson et al. study after they returned to their own neighborhood schools on completion of the Follow Through program. A second purpose of the present study was to replicate the Abelson et al. study with a second cohort.

If the entire data base for evaluating the effects of intervention consisted only of the two cohorts just described, there would be cause for concern regarding how such factors as possible self-selection of the experimental samples might be assessed to permit clear interpretation of the study's results. As many reviewers have noted (Bronfenbrenner, 1974; Campbell & Frey, 1970; Campbell & Stanley, 1963), such a problem is a common one in evaluations of special programs. In the present case, however, the data to be collected form part of a larger matrix of supporting information which has been collected over the past nine years and which can be employed to provide independent estimates of the degree to which certain kinds of selectivity may be operating. Considerable test data and information on parental education and occupation exist for both the Head Start and non-Head Start children in the first cohort who began but failed to complete the four-year extended intervention program. Some indication of the nature of effects of attrition during the program can therefore be obtained. Similar information is available for the Head Start and non-Head Start children who entered public schools following the Head Start year. (Since the completion of the extended intervention program, attrition has been minimal and thus presents few interpretational problems.)

Organization of this Report

The first section of this report describes the research design, followed by a section on the nature of selection and attrition effects in the samples. The next section presents data on the academic test performance of children after the termination of all intervention. The final section turns to data on school grades, school attendance and the interview measure. We present data for low income children and for academic measures only. Data on the performance of middle income children who attended Follow Through is available elsewhere (Seitz, Apfel, & Efron, 1976).

I. Method

In the fall of 1967 the Yale research group began a study of kindergarten-aged children who had just completed Head Start (HS) and who were enrolling in a special continuing intervention program, Project Follow Through (FT), in Hamden, Connecticut. At that time, comparison non-Follow Through (NFT) children were also selected from those enrolling in inner city kindergartens in New Haven, Connecticut. Some of these comparison children had been enrolled in Head Start, some had not. Since the FT project was an integrated school with a considerable socioeconomic and racial mixture in its student body, both middle income and lower income, and both black and white NFT children were selected for comparison. (As noted above, only the low income children's data are considered in this report.)

NFT children were obtained by taking one intact kindergarten classroom from each of seven different New Haven schools. Three of these schools served low income neighborhoods from which most of the low income FT children had been recruited; three of the schools served middle income neighborhoods in which many of the middle income FT children also lived. The seventh comparison school was located in a racially and socioeconomically integrated neighborhood, and the population of this school was similarly an integrated one. One kindergarten classroom was selected from each of these schools by asking the principal to choose a typical classroom in his or her school.

Parents of the children in all schools were asked to fill out an information sheet indicating the number of other children in the family, whether the child in the present study had had HS or nursery school experience, and information on parental occupation, education and income. Such information was obtained for all of the FT children and for over 90% of the NFT children. The children were individually tested with the Peabody Picture Vocabulary Test (PPVT) at the beginning and again at the end of the kindergarten year. They also received the group administered "Screening Test of Academic Readiness" (STAR) at these two times. In the following year, the children enrolling in the FT program were tested in the same manner. No new NFT children were

Figure 1

A Summary of the Longitudinal Strategy for Evaluation
of the Long-Term Effects of Intervention

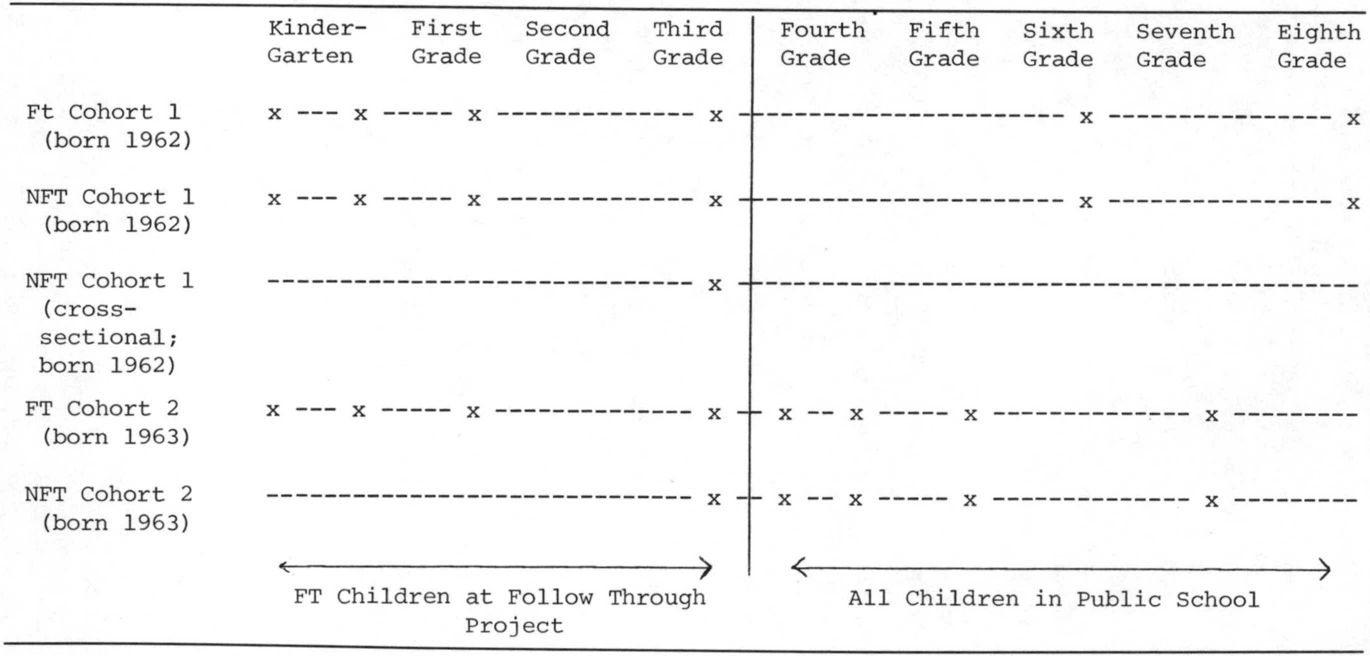

	Kinder-Garten	First Grade	Second Grade	Third Grade	Fourth Grade	Fifth Grade	Sixth Grade	Seventh Grade	Eighth Grade
Ft Cohort 1 (born 1962)	x --- x	-----		------------- x			x	-------	x
NFT Cohort 1 (born 1962)	x --- x	-----		------------- x			x	-------	x
NFT Cohort 1 (cross-sectional; born 1962)				------------- x	-----				
FT Cohort 2 (born 1963)	x --- x	-----		------------- x	-- x	----- x		x	
NFT Cohort 2 (born 1963)				------------- x	-- x	----- x		x	

|← FT Children at Follow Through Project →| |← All Children in Public School →|

x denotes time of testing

tested along with this second cohort of intervention children.

Some data, particularly school administered Metropolitan Achievement Test scores, were gathered for these children during their first and second grade years in school. Extensive retesting was not conducted until the end of the children's third grade year (at which time the FT intervention program was terminating for the children). At the time of the third grade retesting there had been considerable attrition in both cohorts of FT children and in the NFT samples. For this reason, new samples of third grade age NFT children were recruited at the end of the third grade testing of each of the two FT cohorts. These two new comparison samples were limited to low income black children, since the large majority of FT children who completed the program were black and from low income families.

For the first cohort of children, the new cross-sectional control subjects were selected by taking the third grade classmates of the longitudinal control children who could still be located at two of the original four schools from which low income control children had been obtained. (One of these two schools was the integrated school previously described.) Additional cross-sectional control subjects were obtained from an inner city school in another city in Connecticut. This latter group consisted of all children who were of third grade age and who were completing third grade in the newly chosen NFT school. The number of new cross-sectional subjects added was 74; these children were examined only at this one time--no follow-up analyses have been made on these 74 children.

For the second cohort of children, the new cross-sectional control subjects were selected randomly from all children of third grade age who were attending one of the same schools which had provided longitudinal and cross-sectional control children for the first cohort. (The school served an almost all black, all low income population of children in New Haven.) These children have subsequently been studied longitudinally through the seventh grade. Figure 1 summarizes the number of groups studied in the present investigation and the times at which they were tested.

The test administered since third grade has been the Peabody Individual Achievement Test (PIAT) (Dunn & Markwardt, 1970), an individually administered test which requires approximately 45 minutes and which provides measures of mathematics, reading recognition, reading comprehension, spelling and general information, and an overall academic achievement measure based on the sum of the individual parts. The test has the advantage of having been standardized within the past decade on a reasonably representative cross-section of the school population of the United States. The reliabilities of the subtests are satisfactorily high, ranging from .68 to .94 at the third grade level and .61 to .89 at the eighth grade level. The reported median test-retest reliability coefficient for the PIAT tests over the grades involved in the present investigation is .78 (Dunn & Markwardt, 1970). In addition to the PIAT, the children also received the Peabody Picture Vocabulary Test (PPVT) (Dunn, 1965), which provides an estimate of general intellectual ability based upon vocabulary knowledge. The norming of the PPVT is considerably less adequate than that for the PIAT, and the test is probably most useful only in detecting extreme cases of deviation from the average.

In addition to academic testing, a number of linguistic and motivational measures were administered to the Cohort 2 FT and NFT children during fourth grade and to both cohorts of FT and NFT children in the fifth-sixth grade testing. The children from both cohorts have been interviewed during the fifth-sixth grade and the seventh-eighth grade testing periods. The interview requested the child to name his or her favorite thing about school and least favorite thing about school. (Both questions are forced choices to avoid simple socially desirable answers). The child was also asked whether he or she liked school (a question which does have a social desirability problem, but which nevertheless has yielded some interesting findings). As an indirect way of determining personal aspirations and attitudes towards adults, the children were asked to name the grownups they most admired. They were also asked what they thought they would probably be when they grew up and, separately, what they would most like to be if they could be anything they wanted. In addition to the interview, the child's school grades and attendance record have been obtained whenever possible.

II. Selection and Attrition Effects

Several questions are of major interest. First, one may ask how those children who enrolled in the FT program compared on demographic data and test performance with the NFT children from their same neighborhood whose parents chose to send them to their own neighborhood school. This question will be called the selection question. Secondly, one may ask how those children who were still available for study when

they were third graders compared with the children who were
lost from the longitudinal study. This will be called the
attrition question.

Selection

Kindergarten data were obtained on 68 low income FT
children in Cohort 1, on 65 low income FT children in Cohort
2, and 72 low income VFT children in Cohort 1. All of the
children who enrolled at FT at any time during the kindergarten year were included in these samples; almost all of the
low income NFT children enrolling in the four NFT kindergartens (excepting only a few who were absent on scheduled test
days) were included in the sample.

Because subsequent findings in the longitudinal study
have indicated significant sex differences and because selection factors might operate differently for the two sexes,
boys and girls have been treated as separate samples in the
analyses for selection. A separate analysis was also made
for low income black children (who comprise the largest single group in the final longitudinal sample of children).

Individual t-test comparisons were made for each sex
separately to compare the children in each kindergarten
classroom with the children from every other individual
classroom. Such comparisons were made for demographic data
(parental education, the number of siblings, preschool experience) as well as for test performance data (the STAR and
the PPVT). Because of the large numbers of t-tests calculated, the significance levels of the tests on each dependent variable were corrected by multiplying the probability
obtained t-value by the number of comparisons made.

Comparisons between the Cohort 1 FT children and the
Cohort 2 FT children indicated that the two cohorts were
generally comparable. During the first year of the FT program low income girls were more likely than other groups of
low income FT children to come from single parent homes
(almost half were from single parent homes) while in the
second year of the FT program, low income girls came almost
entirely from intact families. This difference was a significant one [$X^2(1)=7.26$, $p<.01$]. For low income boys and
end-of-kindergarten PPVT IQ was significantly higher for the
first cohort than for the second cohort [$\bar{X}=99.8$ versus $\bar{X}=91.2$,
$t(64)=2.50$, $p<.05$]. For low income black children alone no
differences were found in comparing the two cohorts.

Table 1 presents a summary of comparisons of FT with NFT
children. (Although statistical comparisons were made among

Table 1

Differences Between Follow Through and Non Follow Through
Children During the Kindergarten Year
(Low Income Samples Only)

		Boys		Girls	
		black & white	black only	black & white	black only
Age in Months	FT	62.0	61.7	62.6	62.4
	NFT	62.1	62.1	63.7	64.1
Percent w/ HS or Nursery	FT	76***	83***	72***	80***
	NFT	35	35	30	39
Percent from single parent home	FT	30	29	32	27
	NFT	20	13	19	18
No. of Siblings	FT	2.8	2.9	3.0	3.2
	NFT	2.6	2.8	2.7	2.8
Fathers educ. in Years	FT	10.6	10.7	10.1	10.3
	NFT	10.0	9.6	9.5	9.8
Mothers educ. in Years	FT	11.5**	11.5*	10.8	11.0
	NFT	10.3	10.1	10.3	10.4
Star IQ KG Start	FT	90.7	89.6	93.4	90.6
	NFT	94.4	92.3	89.7	87.2
Star IQ KG End	FT	96.6	95.5	99.4	96.7
	NFT	98.9	94.4	94.0	92.0
PPVT IQ KG Start	FT	85.3	82.7	82.2	78.1
	NFT	82.0	77.5	73.0	69.8
PPVT IQ KG End	FT	95.4	94.3	90.2	88.6
	NFT	96.6	93.0	90.1	88.5

*** The FT-NFT difference is significant, $p < .001$
** $p < .01$
* $p < .05$

all individual classrooms--that is, with the two FT cohorts
separately--data in Table 1 are pooled so that the overall
FT-NFT comparison may be seen more clearly.)

Among the low income boys there were three indications
of FT-NFT selection effects: (a) In this sample (as in all
the other low income samples) the FT children were much more
likely to have had HS experience than were the control children. (b) The end-of-year IQs on the STAR instrument were
unusually high at one NFT school ($\overline{X}$=11.7s for the seven low
income boys studies there); this value was significantly
higher than the end-of-year STAR IQ for the Cohort 2 FT boys
and for the boys at one of the NFT schools ($\overline{X}$=94.7 and $\overline{X}$=88.3
respectively). When the average was taken across all
schools, FT children did not differ from NFT children. (c)
For the variable of mother's education, boys at one NFT school
had mothers whose education was significantly lower than that
of the mothers of the boys in the two FT cohorts ($\overline{X}$=9.3
versus $\overline{X}$=11.6 and $\overline{X}$=11.5, respectively). As Table 1 indicates, when data from all NFT school children were pooled the
FT and NFT means differed significantly. When the data were
re-analyzed for the black children alone similar results were
found for the variables of HS experience and mother's education, but the variable of end-of-year STAR IQ was no longer
significant in any group comparisons.

For low income girls only the variable of previous HS
experience was significant. The same was true when the data
were re-analyzed for black children alone.

In summary, there is clear evidence that low income FT
children differed from NFT children in having had the preschool experience of attending a Head Start program. There
is evidence that the mothers of FT boys had somewhat more
education than mothers of NFT boys. The slight evidence for
early IQ differences for the low income boys can perhaps be
discounted since (a) it involved only one of the four low
income NFT schools; (b) it was obtained on one IQ measure,
the STAR, but not on the PPVT; and (c) it was not obtained
when the data were re-analyzed for black children only.
Overall, there appears to be no strong evidence of selection
biases except for whatever factors might lead parents to enroll their children in Head Start.

Attrition

To study attrition the FT children's early test scores
were separated into groups according to whether or not these
children remained at FT for four years and t-test comparisons
were made for each variable to compare the survivors with the

Table 2

Comparison of Children Who Completed Follow Through
With Children Who Left Follow Through (Cohort 1 Only)
(Low Income Samples Only)

	Boys				Girls			
	Black & White		Black Only		Black & White		Black Only	
	Yes[1]	No	Yes	No	Yes	No	Yes	No
Age in Months	---		---		---		---	
Percent with HS or Nursery	95 (N=21)	50** (N=16)	---		---		---	
Percent from Single Parent Home	---		---		---		---	
No. of Siblings	---		---		---		---	
Fathers Educ. in Yrs.	---		---		---		---	
Mothers Educ. in Yrs.	---		11.9 (N=17)	10.8* (N=6)	---		---	
Star IQ, KG Start	---		---		---		---	
Star IQ, KG End	---		---		---		---	
PPVT IQ, KG Start	---		---		---		---	
PPVT IQ, KG End	---		99.8 (N=18)	88.6* (N=5)	---		---	
PPVT IQ, Grade 1 End	---		---		---		95.1 (N=14)	81.2* (N=5)
MET Wd. Kn, Grade 1	---		---		---		---	
MET Wd. Dis, Grade 1	---		---		---		---	
MET Reading, Grade 1	---		---		---		---	
MET Arithmetic, Grade 1	---		---		---		---	
MET Wd. Kn, Grade 2	---		---		---		---	
MET Wd. Dis, Grade 2	---		---		---		---	
MET Reading, Grade 2	---		---		---		---	
MET Arithmetic, Grade 2	---		---		---		---	

** The difference between survivors and nonsurvivors is
   significant, $\underline{p}$ .01
 * $\underline{p}$ .05

---

[1]"Yes" denotes children who completed the FT program;
"No" denotes children who did not.

nonsurvivors. Because of the large number of t-tests made
the significance levels were again adjusted on each variable
by multiplying the probability level of the obtained value by
the number of t-test comparisons made. As before, the data
were examined separately for boys and girls, and separately
for the black children within the low income groups. Unlike
the analysis for the selection question where only kindergarten data were examined, all existing data including first and
second grade achievement scores were examined in studying
attrition.

Examination of the FT low income samples as a whole revealed a relatively high attrition rate of 37% for boys, 51%
for girls, with most of the loss occurring at the end of the
kindergarten year. Much of this loss was due to the exit of
white children from the FT program (approximately 70% of the
low income white children did not remain at the FT program
for the full four years). The rate of attrition for black
low income children alone was less than for all low income
children (74% of the black low income boys and 55% of the
black low income girls who enrolled in kindergarten completed
the full four years of the FT program). The pattern of loss
was also gradual rather than abrupt without the sudden drop
in enrollment at the end of kindergarten seen in the white
sample. The patterns of loss were comparable in Cohort 1 and
Cohort 2.

In the NFT sample, 27 of the 72 original low income
children remained at the end of third grade. Much of this
loss was due, however, to the experimenters' decision to drop
one of the NFT schools from the study when the children were
in first grade because of the introduction of a special tu-
toring program into the school. With the deletion of this
school, the original low income NFT sample had 48 children,
and the percentage of children who were lost was 44%, a figure roughly comparable to the loss in the low income FT samples. Tables 2, 3 and 4 present the results of t-test comparisons between the survivors and nonsurvivors of the Cohort
1 FT sample, the Cohort 1 NFT sample and the Cohort 2 FT sample, respectively.

As Tables 2 and 4 indicate, boys who remained in the FT
program were more likely to have had HS experience than were
boys who left. This finding was not obtained among black
boys alone, however, and may simply reflect the larger attrition among white children. There is some evidence that the
Cohort 2 boys who left the FT program were less capable than
those who remained, while for Cohort 2 the reverse may have
been true. For girls in both cohorts there is some indication that the girls who left the FT program were less academ-

Table 3

Comparison of Non-Follow Through Children
Who Remained in Longitudinal Sample With
Those Who Were Lost (Cohort 1 Only)

(Low Income Samples Only)

	Boys				Girls			
	Black & White		Black Only		Black & White		Black Only	
	Yes[1]	No	Yes	No	Yes	No	Yes	No
Age in Months	---		---		---		---	
Percent with HS or Nursery	---		---		---		---	
Percent from Single Parent Home	---		---		---		---	
No. of Siblings	---		---		---		---	
Fathers Educ. in Yrs.	---		---		---		---	
Mothers Educ. in Yrs.	---		---		---		---	
Star IQ, KG Start	---		---		96.1 (N=14)	80.4* (N=8)	94.5 (N=10)	76.0* (N=7)
Star IQ, KG End	---		---		---		---	
PPVT IQ, KG Start	---		---		---		---	
PPVT IQ, KG End	---		---		---		---	
PPVT IQ, Grade 1 End	---		---		---		---	
MET Wd. Kn, Grade 1	---		---		---		---	
MET Wd. Dis, Grade 1	---		---		---		---	
MET Reading, Grade 1	1.5 (N=8)	1.1* (N=2)	1.5 (N=5)	1.1* (N=2)	---		---	
MET Arithmetic Grade 1	---		---		---		---	
MET Wd. Kn, Grade 2	---		---		---		---	
MET Wd. Dis, Grade 2	---		---		---		---	
MET Reading, Grade 2	---		---		---		---	
MET Arithmetic Grade 2	---		---		---		---	

*The difference between the survivors and nonsurvivors is significant, p .05

[1]"Yes" denotes children who remained in the longitudinal sample; "No" denotes children who did not.

Table 4

Comparison of Children Who Completed Follow Through
With Children Who Left Follow Through (Cohort 2 Only)

(Low Income Samples Only)

	Boys				Girls			
	Black & White		Black Only		Black & White		Black Only	
	Yes[1]	No	Yes	No	Yes	No	Yes	No
Age in Months	---		60.8 (N=24)	63.5* (N=10)	---		---	
Percent with HS or Nursery	85 (N=26)	54* (N=13)	---		---		---	
Percent from Single Parent Home	---		---		---		---	
No. of Siblings	---		---		---		---	
Fathers Educ. in Yrs.	---		---		---		---	
Mothers Educ. in Yrs.	---		---		---		---	
Star IQ, KG Start	---		---		---		---	
Star IQ KG End	---		---		---		---	
PPVT IQ KG Start	77.7 (N=24)	91.5* (N=13)	---		---		---	
PPVT IQ KG End	---		---		---		---	
PPVT IQ, Grade 1 End	---		---		---		102.6 (N=10)	89.17* (N=6)
MET Wd. Kn, Grade 1	1.6 (N=20)	1.9* (N=8)	---		---		---	
MET Wd. Dis, Grade 1	1.8 (N=20)	2.3* (N=8)	1.8 (N=18)	2.4* (N=6)	---		---	
MET Reading, Grade 1	---		---		---		---	
MET Arithmetic, Grade 1	1.6 (N=20)	2.0* (N=8)	---		---		---	
MET Wd. Kn, Grade 2	2.2 (N=22)	3.0* (N=4)	---		---		---	
MET Wd. Dis, Grade 2	---		---		---		---	
MET Reading, Grade 2	---		---		---		3.1 (N=10)	2.0* (N=3)
MET Arithmetic, Grade 2	2.5 (N=22)	3.8* (N=4)	2.4 (N=20)	3.7* (N=3)	---		---	

**The difference between survivors and nonsurvivors is
  significant, p .01
 *p .05

[1]"Yes" denotes children who completed the FT program;
"No" denotes children who did not.

Table 5

Mean Values on Demographic Variables and
Early School Performance for the Cohort 1
Low Income Longitudinal Follow Through
and Non-Follow Through Children

Measure	Boys		Girls	
	FT (N=21)	NFT (N=13)	FT (N=14)	NFT (N=14)
Age in Months	62.6	64.0	61.8	65.0
Percent with HS or Nursery	95[a]	23	86[a]	14
Percent from Single Parent Home	24	15	43	15
No. of Siblings	2.6	3.4	3.1	3.2
Fathers Educ. in Yrs.	10.4	8.9	11.1	9.8
Mothers Educ. in Yrs.	11.8[a,b]	9.7	11.2	10.3
Star IQ, KG Start	88.6	81.9	93.1	96.1
Star IQ, KG End	96.4	92.9	101.3	96.7
PPVT IQ, KG Start	90.8[a,b]	69.7	75.4	70.2
PPVT IQ, KG End	101.2[b]	96.5	88.4	84.8
PPVT IQ, Grade 1 End	103.5[b]	95.5[c]	94.2	85.1
MET Wd. Kn, Grade 1	1.7	1.8	1.6	1.6
MET Wd. Dis, Grade 1	1.8	1.8	1.8	1.7
MET Reading, Grade 1	1.6	1.7	1.7	1.5
MET Arithmetic, Grade 1	1.6	1.8	1.6	1.7
MET Wd. Kn, Grade 2	2.5	2.4	2.4	2.5
MET Wd. Dis, Grade 2	2.7	2.9	2.9	2.9
MET Reading, Grade 2	2.3	2.6	2.4	2.6
MET Arithmetic Grade 2	2.7	3.0	2.5	2.9

[a]The difference between the Follow Through and the non-Follow Through children of the same sex is significant at $p < .05$ or better.

[b]The difference between the sexes in the FT samples is significant at $p < .05$ or better.

[c]The difference between the sexes in the NFT sample is significant at $p < .05$.

ically capable than those who remained. In the NFT sample, as Table 3 shows, what few indications of differential loss exist also suggest the loss of the poorer rather than the better students.

In general, however, the major picture conveyed by tables 2-4 is that despite the many measures upon which survivors and nonsurvivors were compared, very few differences emerged. (The exception to this generalization--Cohort 2 low income boys--can probably be ignored because only the black children from this cohort have continued to be studied longitudinally; the NFT comparison group selected for Cohort 2 in third grade were also all black). Furthermore, if these comparisons had been limited to data from the kindergarten year alone, where the testing was supervised by the experimenters and probably more reliable than the school administered achievement test scores, evidence of any selective attrition would have been even less striking.

In general, it seems reasonable to conclude that the FT children who have been studied in the present investigation were relatively typical of inner city New Haven children except for whatever factors had led their parents to enroll them in a prior HS program. Such factors may be important, but in the present study they did not manifest themselves as differences on the many measures investigated with the single exception of maternal education. Examination of attrition suggests that there has been no large or consistent bias which might make the results of the long-term study suspect.

III. Academic Test Performance of Children Following Completion of Intervention

Cohort 1

Early Differences Between the FT and NFT Children in the Longitudinal Sample

Before presenting data for the third through eighth grade performance of the Cohort I children, a key question of interest is how these particular samples of children compared when they were tested in kindergarten, first and second grade. (This is not identical to the attrition question just discussed, though it is related.) Table 5 presents a summary of the results of these early testings.

As Table 5 indicates, FT children were more likely than NFT children to have had HS experience. Also, parents of the FT children tended to have had somewhat more education than parents of the NFT children, with the difference attaining

significance for the boys. FT girls were slightly younger
than were NFT girls, a difference which can probably be ignored. The PPVT IQ score upon entrance into kindergarten was
higher for FT than for NFT boys and remained so through the
first grade testing. These higher PPVT IQ scores for the FT
boys have been previously reported by Abelson (1974) and seem
to reflect the prior HS experience of the FT boys. None of
the groups differed significantly on the STAR IQ measures,
nor did they differ on measures of academic achievement in
grades 1 and 2.

Third--Eighth Grade Performance

Of the 21 FT boys tested in third grade, 17 were located
in sixth grade and two of the lost children were relocated in
eighth grade for a sample of 19. All of the 13 NFT boys were
retested in sixth grade, and 12 of the 13 were tested in
eighth grade. One irregularity in these data is that one NFT
boy refused testing in third grade except on the PPVT. The
analyses are therefore based on an N of 12 for most of the
third grade FT-NFT comparisons. Among the girls, all 14 FT
girls were tested in third, sixth and eighth grades. All 14
NFT girls were tested in third and sixth grade; two children
could not be located in eighth grade resulting in an N of 12.

Although the fluctuations in sample size were small, the
number of children in the sample was also small. For this
reason, methods of analysis which assess change in performance across time (e.g. repeated measures analyses of variance, multivariate analyses of variance) are not reported at
this time. Such methods necessitate choosing between dis-
carding subjects for whom there is missing data or estima-
ting the missing data from existing scores. Two years from
now, at the completion of this study, we plan to estimate
missing data for subjects if they have been located for sufficient testings to permit some confidence in the stability
of their performance. At present we prefer the direct approach of comparing FT and NFT groups by t-tests, even
though this loses some of the power to be had from repeated
measures analyses. We will cautiously reinterpret these
results by making tentative estimates of missing scores based
on the data presently available.

All analyses have been based upon raw scores in the
following manner: each child's raw score performance on a
test was compared with the raw score which he should have
earned based upon his year and month in school when tested.
This procedure avoids potential problems arising from the
fact that some children were tested several months earlier
than other children. It is important to point out that these

expected raw scores were based upon the grade level which was
appropriate for the child as determined by his age and number
of years in school. For example, children who had failed to
be promoted at some point in their school history were nevertheless judged according to the level appropriate for their
age. Table 6 presents a summary of the significance levels
of one-tailed t-test FT-NFT comparisons on each test and at
each testing period. Where the direction of the FT-NFT difference favors the NFT children, a dashed line indicates this
fact.

As may be seen in Table 6, and as previously reported by
Abelson et al (1974), at the completion of the FT program FT
boys scored higher on mathematics, on general information and
on the PPVT IQ than did NFT boys. As Table 6 indicates, this
pattern has remained similar through the subsequent sixth and
eighth grade re-testings.

Because of the slight fluctuations in the sample, the
question reasonably arises as to whether the reported significance levels might be somewhat altered if the entire
original sample had been retested at each time. We have made
tentative estimates of missing data based on the missing
child's performance on occasions when he was tested. For
each test at each test period the child's performance was
converted into a z-score in comparison with the other children of the same sex and experimental group. The average of
these standard score values was then calculated across all
occasions when the child was actually tested. (This procedure might reveal, for example, that the child was consistently one standard deviation above the mean in mathematics
or that he was a consistently below average speller.) The
child's missing score for a given test was then estimated by
converting his estimated standard score on the test he missed
into the equivalent raw score for that test. In this manner
the effects of the loss of an exceptionally capable student
or an exceptionally poor student can be offset to some degree.

When such an estimation procedure is applied to the
third grade data, filling in the missing NFT child's data,
the conclusion generated is that the significance levels for
mathematics and for general information would have been approximately .07 (unchanged) and .05, respectively. For the
sixth grade data, applying this estimation procedure to
generate the missing four children's scores, the significance
levels for mathematics, general information and PPVT IQ would
have been approximately .20, .02 and .02, respectively, had
all the original children been retested. In the eighth grade
the two lost FT boys were highly capable students while the

Table 6

Significance Levels of One-tailed t-test Comparisons
of FT and NFT Low Income Children in Cohort 1

	Grade When Tested		
	Third	Sixth	Eighth
	Boys		
	(N=21 FT)	(N=17 FT)	(N=19 FT)
	(N=12 NFT)	(N=13 NFT)	(N=12 NFT)
Mathematics	.07	.12	.10
Reading Recognition	---a	---	---
Reading Comprehension	---	---	nsb
Spelling	---	---	---
General Information	.07	.007**	.11
Total PIAT	ns	ns	ns
PPVT IQ	.09	.03*	.09
	Girls		
	(N=14 FT)	(N=14 FT)	(N=14 FT)
	(N=14 NFT)	(N=14 NFT)	(N=12 NFT)
Mathematics	ns	ns	.06
Reading Recognition	ns	---	---
Reading Comprehension	ns	---	---
Spelling	ns	ns	ns
General Information	---	ns	ns
Total PIAT	ns	---	---
PPVT IQ	ns	ns	---

[a]Dashed line denotes that the NFT mean was greater than the FT mean, although not significantly so.

[b]ns denotes that the one-tailed t value is greater than .15.

lost NFT boy was an erratic performer good in mathematics and spelling but very poor in general information and reading comprehension. The effects of these losses were such that the apparent loss of the FT superiority in general information is much more likely simply the effect of losing high scoring FT boys and a low scoring NFT boy. The estimated significance levels for mathematics, general information and PPVT IQ become .13, .05 and .05, respectively, when the missing scores are estimated. The remaining measures—reading recognition, reading comprehension, spelling and the total PIAT score—did not show a significant FT-NFT difference in any analysis of actual or estimated data. The best conclusion from these data appears to be that except for some loss in mathematics the pattern of findings for boys reported by Abelson et al. (1974) has remained essentially unchanged five years following the completion of intervention.

For girls, as Table 6 shows, there is little indication that the FT program produced significant gains. The single exception is in mathematics where there appears to be a sleeper effect—the appearance of a borderline significant finding after previous nonsignificant results. The two NFT girls who were lost from the sample were very poor performers in their earlier testings. The consequence of such a loss is therefore to make the NFT group in eighth grade appear better than it probably would have appeared if all children had been tested. The estimated significance level for the FT-NFT mathematics scores is .03, suggesting that this sleeper effect is a genuine one.

To give some idea of the absolute levels of performance we will report data from the most recent testing, that is, from the fifth month of the eighth grade year (8-5). For the boys the mean grade equivalences for FT and NFT boys, respectively were 7-0 versus 6-1 for mathematics, 7-1 versus 7-7 for reading recognition, 7-5 versus 7-4 for reading comprehension, 6-8 versus 7-5 for spelling, 8-2 versus 7-0 for general information, 7-2 versus 6-9 for overall PIAT achievement, and 97.5 versus 89.8 for the PPVT IQ. For the FT and NFT girls the mean grade equivalences were 7-0 versus 5-8 for mathematics, 6-0 versus 6-5 for reading recognition, 6-4 versus 6-9 for reading comprehension, 7-3 versus 6-9 for spelling, 5-3 versus 5-9 for general information, 6-3 versus 6-3 for overall PIAT achievement, and 86.4 versus 92.0 for the PPVT IQ. (These scores correspond directly to Table 6 and do not include estimates of the performance of missing children.)

Taking all the existing considerations in mind at once, it appears that the results reported by Abelson et al. in 1974 are essentially identical five years later. There has been no fade out and there is one indication of a sleeper effect for FT girls in mathematics.

Cohort 2

Preliminary Considerations

While we have not yet had time to examine fully the long-term effects of Head Start experience for the children in the present study, preliminary examination of whether this factor was of sufficient importance to require its consideration in analyzing the Cohort 2 findings led to some surprising results. Despite the very small numbers of children (only 3 of 13 FT girls had not had HS and only 3 of 22 NFT girls had had HS), it was evident that the non-HS girls in both groups performed increasingly poorly over this time on several measures whereas the HS graduates remained consistently higher. If the FT and NFT girls are pooled and redivided on the basis of prior HS experience and ignoring the FT variable (with resulting N's of 13 HS graduates and 22 non-HS graduates), t-test comparisons of these two groups (using two-tailed significance levels) revealed that in third grade the HS graduates were superior in general information (p=.013) and PPVT IQs (p=.05). In fifth grade the HS graduates were significantly higher on general information (p= .002) and also on the total PIAT score (p=.039) and the PPVT IQ (p=.05). In seventh grade the two groups differed on general information (p=.048) and the PPVT IQ (p=.05).

The results for the boys showed no HS effects except for a reversed direction finding favoring non-HS graduates in mathematics. Three of 24 FT boys had not had HS experience while 4 of 22 NFT boys were HS graduates. A comparison of the 25 HS graduates with the 21 non-HS graduates indicated that the HS graduates scored lower in mathematics in the third grade (p=.04) and in seventh grade (p=.008). No other comparisons were significant.

Because of these differences it was clear that HS attendance could not be ignored in evaluating the results for Cohort 2. For this reason the decision was made for the Cohort 2 sample to compare only those children who had had extensive intervention (HS plus FT) with those children who had had no intervention at all. (In Cohort 1 similar comparisons of HS graduates with non-HS graduates regardless of FT experience had yielded no significant effects for either boys or girls, a result consistent with the earlier findings of Abelson et al., 1974.)

Third--Seventh Grade Performance

Of the 21 FT Cohort 2 boys tested in third grade 20 were
re-tested in fifth grade and again in seventh grade. (One of
these boys, however, refused testing on all but the PPVT and
the mathematics test in seventh grade; some analyses in the
seventh grade are therefore based on an $\underline{N}$ of 20, others on an
$\underline{N}$ of 19.) Of the 18 NFT boys 17 were tested in fifth grade
and again in seventh grade. Among the girls, all 10 FT girls
were tested each time. Of the 19 NFT girls, 18 were tested
in fifth grade and 17 in seventh grade. The girl who was
lost in fifth grade was relocated in seventh grade so that
the two girls lost in seventh grade were lost for the first
time. All of the control girls, therefore, participated in
at least two test periods.

Table 7 presents a summary of the significance levels of
one-tailed $\underline{t}$-test FT-NFT comparisons on each test and at each
testing period. As before, where the direction of the FT-NFT
difference favors the NFT children a dashed line indicates
this fact.

As may be seen in Table 7 the FT boys in Cohort 2 showed
no evidence of positive effects. There was, in fact, one
significant finding which favored the NFT boys on mathematics
in grade seven. All other FT-NFT differences were non-signi-
ficant, with the direction generally favoring the NFT boys.

The picture was very different for the girls. As Table
7 shows, at the end of grade three FT girls were significantly superior to NFT girls in mathematics, general information
and PPVT IQ score. Two years later they not only continued
to be superior to NFT girls on these same measures but they
also scored significantly higher on spelling and on the total
PIAT score. There is thus some evidence for a sleeper effect
for these girls. The seventh grade data do not show any continuation of a sleeper trend, but neither do they suggest
much loss or change in the original pattern of results.

Again the question of the effects of subject loss a-
rises. If an estimate is made for the scores of the one
missing NFT girl in grade five the $\underline{p}$ values become .09 for
mathematics, .06 for spelling, .005 for general information,
.07 for the total PIAT and .03 for the PPVT IQ. This pattern
continues to indicate the sleeper effect for spelling and the
total PIAT score and the persistence of the other significant
findings. In grade seven if estimates are made for the
scores of the two missing control girls the significance
levels become .075 for mathematics, .04 for general information, .09 for the total PIAT score and .065 for the PPVT IQ
score.

Table 7

Significance Levels of One-tailed $\underline{t}$-test Comparisons
of FT and NFT Low Income Children in Cohort 2

	Grade When Tested		
	Third	Fifth	Seventh
	Boys		
	(N=21 FT) (N=18 NFT)	(N=20 FT) (N=17 NFT)	(N=20 FT) (N=17 NFT)
Mathematics	---[a]	---	---
Reading Recognition	---	---	ns[b]
Reading Comprehension	ns	ns	---
Spelling	---	---	---
General Information	---	---	---
Total PIAT	---	---	---
PPVT IQ	---	ns	---
	Girls		
	(N=10 FT) (N=19 NFT)	(N=10 FT) (N=18 NFT)	(N=10 FT) (N=17 NFT)
Mathematics	.035*	.04*	.06
Reading Recognition	---	ns	ns
Reading Comprehension	---	ns	ns
Spelling	ns	.05*	ns
General Information	.01**	.002**	.06
Total PIAT	ns	.045*	.10
PPVT IQ	.01**	.025*	.09

[a]Dashed line denotes that the NFT mean was greater than the FT mean; the difference was significant in one case (mathematics in seventh grade, boys).

[b]ns denotes that the one-tailed $\underline{t}$ value is greater than .15.

In terms of absolute levels of performance we report results from the most recent testing in the fifth month of the
seventh grade year (7-5). For the FT and NFT boys, respectively, mean grade equivalency scores were 4-9 versus 5-3 for
general information, 4-8 versus 5-3 for overall PIAT achievement and 86.8 versus 89.4 for PPVT IQ. For FT and NFT girls,
respectively, the mean grade equivalencies were 7-9 versus
6-6 for mathematics, 7-1 versus 6-2 for reading recognition,
6-6 versus 5-9 for reading comprehension, 7-4 versus 7-1 for
spelling, 6-9 versus 5-8 for general information, 6-9 versus
6-1 for overall PIAT achievement, and 93.4 versus 84.1 for
PPVT IQ. (These scores correspond directly to Table 7 and do
not include estimates of the performance of missing children.)

Comparison of the Results from the Two Cohorts
and General Discussion

When considering the results from both cohorts one
apparently puzzling inconsistency is that it was the FT boys
who were superior to their NFT comparison group in Cohort 1
whereas it was the FT girls who were superior to the NFT
group in Cohort 2. It may be helpful in examining this
matter to refer to Table 8 which presents a summary comparison of differences between the sexes within each FT cohort
and a comparison of the two cohorts. It may also be helpful
to refer back to Table 5 which presents FT-NFT comparisons.

As tables 5 and 8 show there is some indication that the
boys in Cohort 1 (both FT and NFT) were brighter than the
girls and that the FT Cohort 1 boys came from homes which
were more likely to be intact and where the mother was more
educated than was true for the FT girls. There may, therefore, have been a sampling problem, one which affected both
the FT and NFT samples in the case of the IQ data. The fact
that the differences in IQ were confined to the PPVT instrument, however, and did not manifest themselves on other tests
including the STAR IQ measure makes the argument for original
sampling differences favoring boys somewhat tenuous. In the
second cohort it is noteworthy that differences between the
sexes did not begin to emerge until grade one. It does not,
therefore, appear in Cohort 2 that the girls were initially
any more capable than the boys, but rather that they were
more responsive to the effects of intervention. Perhaps the
most likely explanation of the sex differences in the findings for the two cohorts is to be found in the fact that the
Cohort 1 children when tested in third grade were confined to
academic survivors while the Cohort 2 children were not.
Such a fact might well be responsible for the reversed direction of sex effects found in the two cohorts. For example,
girls--who are less likely to be behavior problems in the

Table 8

Mean Values on Demographic Variables and
Early School Performance for the Low Income
Follow Through Samples Studied Since Third Grade

Measure	Cohort 1		Cohort 2	
	Boys (N=21)	Girls (N=14)	Boys (N=21)	Girls (N=10)
Percent from Single Parent Home	24	43	24	10
No. of Siblings	2.6	3.1	3.0	2.4
Fathers Educ. in Yrs.	10.4	11.1	11.0	10.3
Mothers Educ. in Yrs.	11.8[b]	11.2	11.4	11.6
Star IQ, KG Start	88.6	93.1	93.3	91.1
Star IQ, KG End	96.4	101.3	94.4	105.0
PPVT IQ, KG Start	90.9[a,b]	75.4	78.9	88.9
PPVT IQ, KG End	101.2[a,b]	88.4	92.0	93.0
PPVT IQ, Grade 1 End	103.5[a,b]	94.2[c]	93.5[b]	103.6
MET Wd. Kn, Grade 1	1.7	1.7	1.5	1.9
MET Wd. Dis, Grade 1	1.8	1.8	1.8[b]	2.4
MET Reading, Grade 1	1.6[a]	1.7	1.3[b]	1.7
MET Arithmetic, Grade 1	1.6	1.7	1.5	2.0
MET Wd. Kn, Grade 2	2.5	2.4	2.1[b]	2.8
MET Wd. Dis, Grade 2	2.7	2.9	2.5	3.4
MET Reading, Grade 2	2.3	2.4[c]	2.4[b]	3.1
MET Arithmetic, Grade 2	2.7[a]	2.5	2.3	3.0

[a]Difference between the means of the boys in the two cohorts is significant, $p \leq .05$ or better.

[b]Difference between the sexes within the cohort is significant, $p < .05$ or better.

[c]Difference between the means of the girls in the two cohorts is significant, $p < .05$ or better.

classroom--may be more likely to be promoted even if their academic performance is of borderline quality whereas boys may be more likely to be retained. The effects of such differential promotion practices would be that boys who academically survive in the first few years of school might be somewhat brighter than the girls in their classrooms.

Whatever the explanation for the different sex effects in the two cohorts it is interesting that the consistent finding in both Cohorts 1 and 2 was that the FT group which showed significant differences did so in the areas of mathematics, general information and PPVT IQ scores. There was also consistency in the failure to find any influence of FT on reading performance.

Perhaps the most important findings in the present investigation were (a) the apparent absence of a "fade out" effect for those groups of intervention children who were significantly ahead of non-intervention children at the end of the program, and (b) the evidence for increasing differences, or a sleeper effect, for girls after the intervention had ceased. This latter effect is a particularly intriguing one since it is precisely the type of effect hoped for in the original implementation of special intervention programs. The implication is that an intervention program can continue to show its effects even after the children have returned to their regular school programs. This finding is consistent with earlier findings of a persistent effect of Head Start through the kindergarten and first grade years even if children received no further intervention, but a loss of this effect by third grade unless the children had received continued intervention beyond HS (Abelson, 1974; Abelson et al., 1974). In the third grade through seventh grade performance of the Cohort-2 girls there appears to be a similar persistence and even an increase in the effects of intervention for at least two years following termination of intervention. Encouragingly, in the present case there does not seem to be a fading out of effects even four years after termination of intervention.

There are some plausible reasons to explain the emergence of a sleeper effect. The first three grades of school, unlike later grades, are concentrated upon the teaching of basic skills; in the later elementary school grades success is based upon the ability of the child to perform these skills and the curriculum concentrates more upon content than method. The effects of intervention might therefore reasonably be expected to be judged more adequately among children in the later elementary school and junior high grades than during the first few years of school. If it is

the case that the Cohort 2 results in the present investigation can more readily be generalized than the results from
Cohort 1 (because the Cohort 2 children contain both academic
successes and failures) the implication is that girls are
more affected by educational intervention than are boys. If
this is the case (the authors very cautiously suggest that it
is) it may be true because the factors which cause low income
boys to perform poorly in school are less easily affected by
school-based intervention than are the factors which cause
low income girls to perform poorly. Such factors as peer
pressure, early school failure and the conviction that academic success is not masculine may mitigate against the success of school-based intervention for boys; for girls intervention may be effective in instilling early self-confidence
and school success which can be continued even after the program has ceased.

IV. Interview Responses, School Grades and School Attendance

The data to be described in this section were primarily
in the form of frequency counts. Chi square analyses, or
Fisher's Exact Test in cases with very small Ns, were employed to compare FT and NFT children of each sex within each
cohort.

Interview Data

Children's responses to the question of whether they
liked school were coded into "yes" versus other answers (e.g.
"no", "sometimes"). Among the Cohort-2 girls the FT children
were significantly less likely to report liking school than
were the NFT girls (50% versus 89%, p=.04 by Fisher's Exact
Test). The comparisons for the remaining groups were not
significant.

Responses to the question concerning the child's favorite thing about school were coded into the following categories: (a) an academic subject; (b) a non-academic subject
                such as woodworking or shop; (c) social activ-
ities; (d) non-specific academic aspects, e.g. "learning";
and (e) "nothing." Because of the small Ns in some categories (a) and (d) were collapsed into a single category of
academic aspects, and (b) and (c) into a single category of
nonacademic aspects. Comparisons of the FT and NFT groups
for each sex by cohort group revealed no significant differences. Very few children responded to this question by saying that there was nothing which they liked about school.
Interestingly, however, all such children were FT graduates.
Pooling across cohorts and sexes 8% of FT graduates replied

that there was no favorite thing about school for them, while 0% of NFT children gave this response (p=.035 by Fisher's Exact Test).

Responses to the question which asked the child to name the worst thing about school were coded into the following categories: (a) an academic subject; (b) a nonacademic subject; (c) social aspects such as children fighting in halls or bathrooms; (d) rules or discipline aspects such as being sent to the principal's office or being required to take showers in gym; and (e) nothing. Because of the small Ns in some categories they were collapsed into (a) (academic aspects) versus (c) and (d) (rules, discipline and social problems). Category (b) was rarely named. Comparisons of FT and NFT groups revealed no significant differences in frequency of naming these two categories. Relatively few children gave a response indicating that nothing was particularly bad about school. Most children who gave this response were NFT children. Collapsing across cohorts and sexes, only 5% of FT children indicated that there was nothing which they felt to be particularly bad about school while 18% of the NFT children gave this response (p=.025 by Fisher's Exact Test).

Children's responses to the question of what grownups the child most admired were coded into the following categories: (a) family members, other relatives or family friends; (b) community leaders; (c) persons in sports or performing arts; (d) teachers; and (e) others. Categories (b) and (e) were rarely mentioned. Analyses were therefore made comparing FT and NFT children with respect to whether or not they mentioned family members and friends among adults they most admired, whether or not they mentioned sports and performing arts persons and whether or not they mentioned teachers. None of these analyses yielded significant results.

The child's career aspiration was graded into socioeconomic status categories on a scale of 1--5 with 1 denoting unskilled, 2 semiskilled, 3 clerical, 4 white collar and managerial and 5 professional occupations. A similar coding was made of the child's response to the question what he would like to be if he could be anything he wanted. Analysis of variance on both the real and the ideal aspiration levels produced no significant results.

Grades and Attendance

On the basis of the child's school grades and his grade level each child's academic success was coded as follows: (a) grossly failing as indicated by the child's having been retained in a lower grade than appropriate for his age or in a special learning disabilities group; (b) at grade level but failing (earning D's and F's); (c) at grade level with mar- ginal to average performance (earning C's and D's); (d) at grade level with average to good performance (earning C's and B's); and (e) superior (above or at grade level, earning A's and B's). Because of small Ns in some groups these categor- ies were collapsed into (a) and (b), failing, versus (c), (d) and (e), adequate or better school performance. Comparisons of FT and NFT groups in each sex by cohort grouping yielded no significant differences in the frequency of representation of FT and NFT children in these categories.

School attendance was categorized as adequate (defined as 0-15 absences during the school year) versus poor (16 or more absences). Comparisons of FT and NFT children yielded no significant differences in school attendance.

Discussion of Findings from Interviews, Grades and School Attendance Data

In summarizing the results from the interview, grades and attendance data it appears that one effect of the FT program has been to lead children to be more critical of their post-FT school experience. Surprisingly, however, a lesser liking for school does not seem to spell itself out in poorer attendance or school grades. In fact, as previously noted, the FT girls in Cohort 2 have consistently been better aca- demic performers on several measures than have the NFT girls, yet these FT girls are particularly likely to report that they do not like school.

It is difficult to gauge what the long-range effects of such feelings might be. Possibly if fade out does eventually occur it may be for this reason. It is also clear from the interview, however, that the intervention children believe that they must be special in some way and they frequently reminisce positively about their early years at FT. The children's reflections seem, in fact, almost nostalgic. Their present tendency to criticize school appears therefore to re- flect an awareness of what a more positive school experience could be. The eventual effects of their attitudes toward school could, of course, be either positive or negative. Their faith in the potentialities of school programs might sustain them through otherwise difficult times. On the other hand, the frustration engendered by the comparison of what might be with what is may eventually lead to a drop in perfor- mance. Two years from now when these same children are in ninth and tenth grades we plan to test them for the final time to determine the effects of the early intervention. At that time we will issue a final report of this study.

Acknowledgements

This research has been supported by Research Grant MN-3008 from the National Institute of Mental Health, U.S. Public Health Service; by Research Grant 90-C-912 from the Office of Child Development, U.S. Department of Health, Education, and Welfare; Grant Number 1876-08330 from the Education Commission of the States; the Gunnar Dybwad Award of the National Association for Retarded Citizens; and the Follow Through Project of the U.S. Office of Education. The authors wish to express their appreciation to the staffs of the Hamden New Haven Cooperative Education Center and the Hamden and New Haven Public Schools for their cooperation and assistance.

Many persons have generously contributed towards making the post intervention follow-up research possible. In particular, we wish to thank Robert S. Avery, Director of the Hamden-New Haven Cooperative Education Center; Audrey P. Tiani, Project Coordinator, Project Follow Through; Carol Corso, Hamden-New Haven Cooperative Education Center; Samuel Nash, Director of Special Projects and Planning for New Haven Public Schools; Jessie G. Bradley, Director of Elementary Schools, New Haven Public Schools; Gerald N. Tirozzi, Director of Middle Schools, New Haven Public Schools; Edward Mas, Superintendent, Hamden Public Schools, James J. Sullivan, Director of Parochial Schools, New Haven; Garyce Dowdy, Director of Head Start Programs, New Haven; Lorraine Celentano of the New Haven Public Schools; Elizabeth Levine of the New Haven Prekindergarten Program; and the many principals, teachers and guidance counselors and others who assisted in the location of the children in these samples. We also thank Elizabeth Katz who tested the Cohort 2 children in third and fourth grades; Sammy Carr and Cheryl LaRossa who assisted extensively with data preparation; and Karen Anderson who aided immeasurably with scoring and computer analyses, Bridget Thomsen for clerical assistance with the manuscript, Jane Edmister for assistance in preparation of graphics, and Linda Hughes for editorial assistance and for typing.

References

Abelson, W.D. Head Start graduates in school; Studies in New Haven, Connecticut. In S. Ryan (Ed.), A report on longitudinal evaluations of preschool programs. Vol. 1. Longitudinal evaluations. Washington, D.C.: Department of Health, Education and Welfare, Publication No. (OHD) 74-24, 1974.

Abelson, W.D., Zigler, E., & DeBlasi, C. Effects of a four-year Follow Through program on economically disadvantaged children. Journal of Educational Psychology, 1974, 66, 7560771.

Bronfenbrenner, U. A report on longitudinal evaluations of preschool programs. Vol. 2. Is early intervention effective? Washington, D.C.: Department of Health, Education and Welfare, Publication No. (OHS) 74-25, 1974.

Campbell, D.T., & Erlebacher, A. How regression artifacts in quasi-experimental evaluations can mistakenly make compensatory education look harmful. In J. Hellmuth (Ed.), Compensatory education: A national debate. Vol. III of the disadvantaged child. New York: Brunner/Mazel, 1970.

Campbell, D.T., & Frey, P.W. The implications of learning theory for the fade-out of gains from compensatory education. In J. Hellmuth (Ed.), Compensatory education: A national debate. Vol. III of the disadvantaged child. New York: Brunner/Mazel, 1970.

Campbell, D.T., & Stanley, J.C. Experimental and quasi-experimental designs for research. Chicago: Rand Mc Nally, 1963.

Dunn, L.M. Peabody Picture Vocabulary Test. Minneapolis, Minn.: American Guidance Service, 1965.

Dunn, L.M., & Markwardt, F.C. Peabody Individual Achievement Tests. Circle Pines, Minn.: American Guidance Service, 1970.

Horowitz, F.D., & Paden, L.Y. The effectiveness of environmental intervention programs. In B.M. Caldwell & H.N. Riccuiti (Eds.), Review of Child Development Research. Vol. 3. Chicago: University of Chicago Press, 1973.

Ryan, S. (Ed.), A report on longitudinal evaluations of preschool programs. Vol. 1. Longitudinal evaluations. Washington, D.C.: Department of Health, Education and Welfare, Publication No. (OHD) 74-24, 1974.

Seitz, V. Integrated versus segregated school attendance and immediate recall for standard and nonstandard English. Developmental Psychology, 1975, 11, 217-223.

Seitz, V., Abelson, W.D., Levine, E., & Zigler, E. Effects of place of testing on the Peabody Picture Vocabulary Test scores of disadvantaged Head Start and non-Head Start children. Child Development, 1975, 46, 481-486.

Seitz, V., Apfel, N.H., & Efron, C. Long-term effects of

intervention: A longitudinal investigation. Paper presented at the 84th Annual Convention of the American Psychological Association, Washington, D.C., September, 1976.

Smith, M.S., & Bissell, J.S. Report analysis: The impact of Head Start. Harvard Educational Review, 1970, 40, 51-104.

Stanford Research Institute. Implementation of planned variation in Head Start: Preliminary evaluation of planned variation in Head Start according to Follow-Through approaches (1969-70). Washington, D.C.: Department of Health, Education and Welfare, Office of Child Development, 1971 (a).

Stanford Research Institute. Longitudinal evaluation of selected features of the national Follow-Through program. Washington, D.C.: Department of Health, Education and Welfare, Office of Education, 1971 (b).

Westinghouse Learning Corporation. The impact of Head Start experience: An evaluation of the effects of Head Start on children's cognitive and affective development. Vol. 1. Text and Appendices A-E. Ohio University Report to the Office of Educational Opportunity, Clearinghouse for Federal, Scientific and Technical Information, Washington, D.C., 1969.

Zigler, E., Abelson, W.D., & Seitz, V. Motivational factors in the performance of economically disadvantaged children on the Peabody Picture Vocabulary Test. Child Development, 1973, 44, 294-303.

The Developmental Continuity Consortium Study

4

Secondary Analysis of Early Intervention Data

Virginia Ruth Hubbell

In July 1976, the U.S. Office of Child Development awarded a grant to the Education Commission of the States, which in turn contracted with eight principal investigators who had conducted early educational intervention studies in the mid-1960's to enable them to pool their existing original data and to locate their original subjects and assess their current life situation. OCD also directly supported three additional investigators. All these individuals have joined together to form the Developmental Continuity Consortium, which is coordinated by Dr. Irving Lazar and his staff at Cornell University. The members of the Consortium are Dr. Kuno Beller, Temple University; Drs. Cynthia and Martin Deutsch, New York University; Dr. Phyllis Levenstein, Verbal Interaction Project, Freeport, New York; Dr. Merle Karnes, University of Illinois; Dr. Louise Miller, University of Louisville; Dr. Frank Palmer, University of New York - Stonybrook; Dr. David Weikart, High/Scope Foundation; Dr. Myron Woolman, Education Research Institute, Washington, D.C.; Dr. Edward Zigler, Yale University. These eleven individuals have directed the fourteen studies which are the basic data of the Developmental Continuity project.

The purposes of the Consortium are to pool the original data from the individual studies, and to coordinate the investigators' efforts in the current follow-up studies of their original subjects.

The Developmental Consortium operation represents the first time that this original raw data has been made available to a single research source for analysis. By pooling the data it will be possible for the sample size to be raised dramatically over the size available to any single investigator. This increased size will increase the power of the statistical analyses in the testing of hypotheses and in heuristic searches for significant relationships between

111

demographic variables, intervention, and outcome measures.

The studies involved in the Consortium effort encompass a broad range of early childhood intervention approaches. A variety of staffing patterns, curricula, and delivery systems were used by the studies. The studies were located in different regions of the country, and intervened at different points in early childhood. However, all dealt with similar (disadvantaged) populations.

The fourteen studies are primarily concerned with the effects of pre-school educational intervention on the level of cognitive performance of the participating children. To a lesser, but still important degree, they are also concerned with the effects of the intervention on the children's socio-emotional development, on the parents, and on the improvement of their home environments.

The studies may be viewed from the perspective of the object of intervention - the child, the parent or the parent-child dyad. This perspective is consistent with the type of primary delivery system utilized by the programs, center-based or home-based. The center-based programs, including those designed by Beller, Gray, Karnes, Miller, Palmer, Weikart, Deutsch and Zigler, were directed at determining the effects of group, child-centered intervention. Several of the center-based programs, (Gray, Miller, and Weikart), also had some type of parental intervention in addition to the center-based program. The home-based programs, including work by Gray, Weikart, Gordon and Levenstein, were directed primarily at attempting to improve the parents' abilities as teachers of their children.

All of the studies used samples consisting of children and their families who had low socio-economic status, low educational levels, poor housing conditions, low income levels, were heavily Black, and often were headed by only one parent.

The following descriptions of each study were developed in 1976. There have been a few more recent follow-up studies performed by individual investigators which were not then available. Some of these more current findings are included in the research reports by those investigators in their papers in this volume.

Center-based Programs

There are two major types of center-based programs. First are those which studied the effects of one specific intervention curriculum model in comparison to a control group. Second are those which studied the effects of variations of different curricula on the children. Single-model intervention studies were conducted by Zigler, Gray, and Deutsch; multiple-model programs were studied by Karnes, Miller, Palmer, Beller, and Weikart.

Single-Model Intervention

Zigler investigated the effects of regular Head Start and Follow Through interventions on two cohorts of preschool children in New Haven, Connecticut. In 1967, Zigler's first cohort of children, who had just completed Head Start and were beginning Follow Through, were chosen along with a non-head Start control group who were enrolling in regular public kindergarten. Follow-up testing on measures of academic achievement, IQ, and socio-emotional development after the third grade showed the Follow Through children to be significantly higher on all of these measures than the control children. Sixth grade follow-up also showed significant differences in IQ, general information and mathematics achievement.

The second cohort did not show experimental group superiority at the end of the third grade but did show significant differences from the control group at the end of the fifth grade on tests of reading recognition, spelling, and general information.

Further follow-up information is being collected on such variables as social, motivational, and linguistic development, and plans are being made to include more global evaluations of social and personality factors as the children move into adolescence.

Cynthia and Martin Deutsch also examined the effects of one specific intervention program on four sample waves of children from low-income areas in New York City. They compared these to control children from the same areas. Their specifically developed curriculum (which began with a preschool program and extended into the elementary school through the third grade) emphasized language development, concept formation, perceptual and overall cognitive development, and the child's self-concept. Significant differences between the experimental and control groups were found on the Stanford-Binet after kindergarten, and on the Peabody Picture Vocabulary Test after the third grade. Significant differences were also found on achievement tests and on the Illinois Test of PsychoLinguistic Abilities at the end of the third grade.

The Early Training Project conducted by Dr. Susan Gray utilized a single intervention model, but implemented it through two delivery systems, a center-based summer program and a home visitor winter program. The program was directed towards developing the child's attitudes and aptitudes conducive to school success, as well as his general compe-tence, and towards encouraging the parent to become a more effective teacher of the child. Two cohorts of children were involved. Significant differences between experimental and control group children were found through the second grade on intelligence tests, language tests, and school achievement. Significant differences on intelligence tests through the fourth grade were found to favor the experimental children. Achievement test scores were also higher for the experimental children, although differences were not significant.

Kuno Beller of Temple University studied the effects of variations in the timing of entrance into preschool or school on a variety of measures. Three groups of children were involved; one entered an experimental nursery school at age four, one entered public kindergarten at age five, and one simply entered first grade at age six. An extensive battery of tests was administered to all of the children. Significant differences between the experimental and control subjects were found on IQ tests through the fourth grade, and on academic achievement measures of reading, spelling, science and social studies through fourth grade. Significant differences among the three groups were found on autonomous achievement striving and on aggression in the first grade. Autonomous achievement striving in the first grade was found to correlate significantly with intelligence test scores, and with academic achievement in the fourth grade.

David Weikart's Perry Preschool Project, begun in 1962, provided 58 academically high-risk children with a cognitively-oriented preschool program for two years before the children entered kindergarten. Five cohorts of children were studied over a period of thirteen years. Results showed that preschool attendance had an immediate and positive impact on the measured cognitive-linguistic development of the children in the experimental group. The magnitude of differ-ences between the experimental and control groups decreased somewhat following school entrance, but significant differ-ences on the California Achievement Test were still maintained at the end of second grade. Similarly, the proportion of experimental children who were at their appropriate grade level at the end of the fourth grade was significantly higher than that of the control group. Weikart also found increasing magnitude of differences on the ratings of socio-emotional maturity between the experimental and control children through the fourth grade.

Dr. Myron Woolman studied the effects of a preschool program called the Micro-Social Laboratory on 135 children in Vineland, New Jersey. Over 90% of the children came from low-income, migrant farm worker families, and 65% of the children were Spanish-speaking. The Micro-Social Laboratory program utilized an arrangement of modular units in which children worked through a pre-planned series of activities in pairs, receiving periodic reinforcement as they completed each objective in a sequence. The program design also included a life-simulator space in which the children applied their newly learned skills in free play.

After eight months in the program, Woolman found significant Wechsler IQ gains of over 9 points among the E's. Gains in IQ for 80% of the sample were also found on a study developed Learning Effectiveness Scale.

Multiple Model Programs

Palmer, Karnes, Miller and Weikart all studied the effects of varying the curriculum within the center-based model. Using primarily the same varieties of curricula, the four separate studies have shown similar results.

Frank Palmer considered the differences between two models: a Concept Training group and a Discovery group. The subjects were 310 Black 2- and 3-year old boys from the Harlem section of New York City. The experimental children attended the Concept Training or Discovery program for one hour, twice weekly, for eight months. Following the completion of the training, significant differences were found between the experimental and control group children on measures of IQ, concept familiarity, simple perceptual discrimination, motor performance, and labeling. There were no significant differences between the two experimental groups except on concept familiarity favoring the concept training group. This increase of course, was precisely the objective of the concept training curriculum. Assessments of the children at age four did not show any significant differences between experimentals and the control group. However, at the age of ten, a sample of ninety of the children were retested, and the scores of the experimental children on the Metropolitan Achievement Test were three months ahead of the median score in their schools. The IQ test scores of the experimental group subjects were also considerably higher than those normally reported for Black male children in the third grade.

The studies of Karnes, Miller and Weikart are most

similar in the study of multiple curricula models. All three
of these studies selected the Bereiter-Engelmann curriculum
as one model, a cognitively-oriented, moderately structured
program (Karnes' "Ameliorative," Miller's "Demonstration and
Research Center for Early Education" (DARCEE) Program and
Weikart's "Cognitive Training") as another, and a "traditional" nursery school program variation as well. Karnes and
Miller also had Montessori programs, and Karnes additionally
had a community-integrated group.

Merle Karnes' five groups of children (a total of 75
children) were all four-year-olds from the Champaign-Urbana,
Illinois area. Each group attended one of the ·preschool
models for about two and one quarter hours a day for seven to
eight months. Following the period of intervention, there
were no statistically significant differences among the five
groups on the PPVT. However, the Bereiter-Engelmann and
Ameliorative program groups were significantly higher than
the Montessori and community-oriented groups, but not significantly higher than the traditional group on the Stanford-
Binet. At the end of kindergarten, the Bereiter-Engelmann
group was superior on the Stanford-Binet and the ITPA, but
the Ameliorative group was superior on the Metropolitan Reading Readiness Test. At the end of first grade, the Bereiter-
Engelmann and Ameliorative groups were still significantly
ahead in reading readiness and arithmetic.

Louise Miller's four groups, Bereiter-Engelmann, DARCEE,
Traditional and Montessori, attended half-day Head Start
programs at age four, followed by two types of kindergarten
programs at age five. At the end of the Head Start year,
significantly greater IQ's were found for those children
exposed to the two most didactic, academic programs -
Bereiter-Engelmann and DARCEE. However, the combination of
Bereiter-Engelmann prekindergarten followed by a regular non-
academic kindergarten was disastrous for academic achievement.
For DARCEE prekindergarten, there was little difference in
academic achievement as a function of the type of kindergarten
which followed. The combination of non-academic pre-kindergarten and an academic kindergarten produced good results.
Over the succeeding two-year (1st and 2nd grade) period, in
various follow-up programs, the Bereiter-Engelmann children
decreased more in IQ than children from the other three
programs.

David Weikart's Curriculum Demonstration Study Research
in Ypsilanti, Michigan, utilized three curricula: Bereiter-
Engelmann, cognitive training, and a unit-based or traditional model. The children attended a half day program and were
visited once a week by a teacher for a 90 minute period of

instruction and continuity for two years. Gains during the
initial year for three waves of children in the program
ranged from 17 to 30 points on the Stanford-Binet, and these
gains were equally large from all three models. Although
there was some decline after the children entered kindergarten and elementary school, the substantial gains held up
through the end of second grade. Similar results were also
found on the California Achievement tests at the end of
second grade.

Home-based Programs

The three home-based programs in which the parent or the
parent-child dyad was the target of intervention were quite
similar in their focus, technique, and research design. All
utilized staff members who went into the family's home on a
regular basis to interact with the mother in an effort to
improve her parenting skills. While the specific curriculum
emphasis differed somewhat from program to program, it was
generally centered around this similar goal. A unique,
original curriculum was utilized by each of the three programs, with variations of that treatment being provided to
the various experimental and control groups. An important
difference among the programs involved the use of professional or paraprofessional staff members.

Ira Gordon's Parent Education program at the University
of Florida was specifically focused on the enhancement of the
intellectual and personality development of the child and the
production of changes in the mother's self-esteem and conviction that she could affect what happened to herself and her
child. Gordon utilized trained paraprofessional home
visitors who visited the mother once a week. The sequenced
curriculum emphasized Piagetian concepts appropriate to the
child's stage of development. One treatment group received
weekly visits for two years, starting at age 3 months; a
second, visits from 3 months to a one year; and a third,
visits for one year to age two years. A control group received testing only. Significant differences were found
between experimental and control groups at age one, no differences at age two, a recurrence of differences at 27 months,
and stronger and more consistent differences at age four,
favoring the experimental treatment, which provided intervention for two or three consecutive years on the Stanford-Binet,
PPVT, and Leiter International Picture Vocabulary test.

As the children in the Parent Education Project reached
2 years of age, they entered Gordon's Home Learning Center
program. This treatment continued weekly home visits to the
parent, but added a twice-weekly 4-hour group experience for

five children at a time. The home or "backyard center" was
the home of a mother in the project, and activities were
directed by a former parent educator. This segment of the
program lasted for a year. Gordon found that the experimental
group children who had been in the combination of programs
for three years were statistically superior to the control
group on the Stanford-Binet at ages 3, 4, 5, and 6.

Dr. Susan Gray also operated a home-based program. Her
major purpose was to enable parents to become more effective
agents of education change with their small children. In
fact, the entire family was seen as a change agent, and any
family members present during the home visit were included in
the activities. The curriculum emphasized infant growth and
development in the physical and psycho-social areas of the
infant's functioning. Home visitors in the "Extensive Home
Visiting" treatment visited the homes for at least one hour
per visit for a maximum of 24 visits. A "Materials Only"
condition group received the same written instructions and
materials, but were staffed by volunteers. At the end of
ten months of training, the families were randomized into two
groups for either continued contact once a month or for no
sustained contact. Gray found immediate post-test differences
on only one test, the receptive language instrument, but
after two years found (similar to Gordon) significant differences on the Stanford-Binet and on the Maternal Teaching
Strategy Instrument favoring the experimental group.

Levenstein utilizes a "toy demonstrator" concept to
provide experimental treatment to the subjects of her Verbal
Interaction Project, conducted in Freeport, Long Island. The
purpose of the program is to prevent educational disadvantage
in low-income populations through early cognitive-affective
intervention. The main technique for the accomplishment of
this objective is to enhance the verbal interaction between
the mother and the child. Since 1967, Levenstein has utilized a variety of treatment conditions, with systematic
variance of many key variables. However, her primary treatment groups consist of an experimental group that receives
half-hour weekly visits from social worker home visitors who
"demonstrate" a series of toys to the mothers for interaction
with the child; a second group receives the sequenced materials only, and a third non-instructional group gets visits
only. A control group only receives testing. Large gains up
to 17 IQ points have been manifested by the experimental
groups on the PPVT. Significant differences were maintained
at least two years following termination of treatment despite
small decreases in IQ scores during subsequent follow-up
testings.

Weikart also instituted a home-based infant program in collaboration with Lambie and Bond. The program's curriculum emphasized the developmental theory of Piaget and stressed the facilitation of the growth of mothers as teachers. It provided a Piagetian theory based series of lessons to very young infants and their parents in their homes. The children were in three cohorts of ages 3, 7 and 11 months at pre-tests. All families were low-income and low SES. The subjects were randomly assigned to treatment, contrast and control groups. The treatment group received weekly home visits by a professional teacher; the contrast group received weekly visits from a volunteer student or community person trained in child care; and the control group received testing only.

The program lasted for 16 months. On the Bayley Infant Scales and Stanford-Binet Intelligence Tests, Weikart found that the infants from the experimental group performed at a significantly higher level than did contrast or control groups at the post-test. He also found experimental group mothers scored significantly higher than did the control group on a measure of verbal interaction between mother and child at post-test.

Methodological Considerations

Despite the apparent similarity of these studies, the challenges encountered combining them in a common pool have been extensive. It has only been through the determined and persistent efforts of Research Associate Harry Murray, other staff members and consultants at Cornell, and advice from Consortium members that satisfactory resolutions of these problems have been found.

However, acknowledgment of the discrepancies and problems should not be misinterpreted. The present staff members find ourselves in the position of secondary analyzers who

> enjoy advantages that a primary evaluation
> researcher does not have. If the latter are
> like the brave men in front-line trenches
> who are pushing us towards a self-monitoring
> society in the face of numerous difficulties,
> then university secondary analysts might be
> likened to "Monday-morning generals." (1)

We are in the position of attempting to analyze data which was not collected in order to be comparable to that collected by other studies, but to examine the effects of various interventions for a variety of objectives. Thus some of the analyses must be somewhat more "tortured" than they would have been, had the studies been concurrent replications of each other, or one massive study. Of course, if that had been the case, we might not have the rich diversity of approaches that are available for examination.

Given these caveats, we may turn to the main sources of non-comparability which are found in the various research designs and instrumentation used across studies.

All of the studies may be classified as quasi-experimental designs. All but one had control groups; several had contrast groups. However, such factors as pre-testing, random assignment of subjects to experimental or control groups, and time of post-testing vary considerably from study to study.

Pre-testing varied from those studies which pre-tested before the intervention program began to those which pre-tested after the children had been in the intervention program for a few weeks, and had become more at ease with strange adults. The latter approach has been found to yield higher test scores.

As each study focused upon a different age group, (some were infants, some 2, 3 or 4 year olds) the age of the children at pre-test also varied, thus complicating comparisons across studies at pre-test. In addition, the tests used at pre-test differed within as well as across studies. For example, standard procedures in a particular study may have been to administer the Stanford-Binet to subjects at intake. However, if the subject was not mature enough for the Stanford-Binet, the Cattell or Bayley may have been administered instead. Thus pre-tests on the Stanford-Binet would be available for only the more advanced children.

Studies varied as to whether children were pre- and post-tested at a particular age, or at a particular time of the year. To deal with this problem, time spans were developed into which testing periods were grouped. For example, children tested anywhere between 18 months and 24 months of age were grouped into one testing span.

Random assignment was achieved by most studies. However, in some cases assignment to experimental or control groups was made by random assignment of intact groups of subjects or by assignment to groups by matching of individuals. In some cases, subjects were randomly assigned to experimental or control groups, in other cases control groups were obtained separately or were obtained from waiting lists for programs. In all cases, parents of subjects had to elect to participate in the program.

The time of post-testing varies as did pre-testing. The situation was further complicated by the fact that as studies depleted their research funds, follow-up testing was curtailed. Thus, follow-up post-testing was rarely performed for more than four years after the conclusion of the intervention, as is reflected in the summaries above. Therefore, for those studies which dealt with infants, no comparable post-tests exist at the same ages as for the programs which intervened with older children. In some cases the younger children had simply not reached comparable ages, and in others funds were only available to follow up limited numbers of children, thus creating forced attrition.

Actual attrition also occurred in all projects although to greater and lesser degrees in each study. Extensive attrition analyses are planned to determine whether the subjects remaining in the study at each follow-up period (including the present one) differ significantly from the original samples on both test and demographic variables. (Preliminary analyses of the original data indicate that they do not differ.)

Instrumentation presented a real challenge in the search for comparability. Because the investigators had differing objectives for their studies, and different hypotheses, they used a wide variety of intelligence, socio-emotional, behavioral, and specific cognitive tests. Some of these measures are well-known, widely used instruments (such as the Stanford-Binet Intelligence Test or Peabody Picture Vocabulary Test) while others are more obscure (Dog and Bone) and still others were self-developed (Levenstein's Child Behavior Traits Rating Scale). Indeed, over fifty different instruments were used. Of these only the Stanford-Binet and the PPVT were used by enough studies to make comparisons across studies possible.

The problems inherent in the Stanford-Binet and PPVT are well-known and documented. The Stanford-Binet in particular is a very stable, verbal skill-dependent measure. It may have little relevance to the world of the lower-class Black child who characterizes the consortium's sample. However, it has been established as a fairly good indicator of general intelligence and as a valid predictor of school success, both abilities which our society deems important. (Cronbach, 1960) Therefore, despite their limitations, the Stanford-Binet and PPVT are used in most of the original analyses as the prime dependent variables.

As in the tests used, there were wide discrepancies in the information collected and in the definitions for that information on family and demographic characteristics at the initiation of the studies. Some studies collected only data descriptive of the entire sample based upon neighborhood information; others collected comprehensive individual interview data for each subject. One of the first major undertakings of the present study was to reconcile the definitions of the demographic items and put them into a common format so that they could be analyzed jointly. For example, the definition of sibling (and thus the definition of birth order) varied. In some cases it was defined as "Any other child living in the home," in others as "Any other child of the mother." These two definitions were empirically determined to be comparable and were consolidated.

To prevent such problems of non-comparability in the current follow-up study, decisions on the choice of instruments to be used in the present follow-up study evolved from lengthy discussion of the alternatives by the Consortium members which lasted for over six months. Because of financial restrictions and the high cost of locating subjects who had not been interviewed or tested for many years, it was necessary to choose a limited battery of measurements. The Consortium agreed to administer the Wechsler Intelligence Scale for Children-Revised or the Wechsler Adult Intelligence Scale (depending upon the age of the subject) and the Consortium-developed Parent and Youth Interviews, and to obtain data from the achievement tests administered by the schools as well as data from the school records.

The Developmental Continuity Parent Interview was initially developed from a compilation of interviews used by individual investigators, especially those of David Weikart and Martin Deutsch. The interview was pre-tested twice; the second pre-test used a carefully controlled design which included families of children who had attended Head Start in Ithaca, New York, or had participated in a home-based parent education program based in Elmira, New York, from two to ten years earlier. The pre-test sample parents were representative of the actual sample to be interviewed on such variables as race, urban-rural status, and number of years since their child had been in the program.

The Parent Interview is designed to obtain comprehensive information on household composition, socio-economic status, parental attitudes toward, aspirations for, and evaluations of their child, information on the child's medical history, school educational history, the parent's current relationship with the child, and parental assessment of the intervention program.

The Youth Interview also drew upon previously developed interviews used by the Principal Investigators, but it leans more heavily upon terms discussed as being of salient interest to them at several Consortium meetings. This interview was also revised and pre-tested in the manner of the Parent Interview.

The Youth Interview will obtain information on the child's status in school, his educational and occupational aspirations, leisure time activities and interests, heroes employment status, and integration into his peer group and the larger community.

Special efforts were made in both interviews to include items of specific interest to all Principal Investigators, and to avoid inflammatory questions while still obtaining vital sociological information. (For example, the decision was made to delete a question asking if the child had ever had trouble with the police. A question asking for the "worst thing" that had ever happened to the child was substituted.)

Both interviews were disseminated to the studies in October. The projected completion date for the approximated 1,000 subjects to be involved in the follow-up study is April 1, 1977.

These interviews were produced as the result of extensive work by Jacqueline Royce and the author of this paper. They should provide rich descriptions of the current, past and hoped-for lives of an important sub-group of the U.S. population.

Another instrument comparability problem is to be confronted with the analysis of the achievement test data. Because of the lack of funds it was not possible to administer individual achievement tests. Therefore, as the hundreds of schools attended by the subjects use a variety of tests, comparison will have to be made across tests as well as across subjects and studies. Despite the fact that most widely used national achievement tests were standardized on large samples, raw scores, percentiles and standard scores which should theoretically be directly comparable actually are not. The Anchor Study (Loret et al., 1974) found 13 point differences between supposedly equivalent raw scores and a study by Millman and Lindlof (1964) found up to 6% differences between equivalent percentiles.

While the Anchor Test study does provide conversion tables for eight tests, these conversions are available only

Table I. Pooled Z's and Significance for t-tests by # Years after Treatment Termination

	significance level at immediate posttest	significance level at 1 yr. after treatment	significance level at 2 yrs. after treatment	significance level at 3 or 4 yrs. after treatment
Gordon *	.072	.022	.018	.007
ETP	.0001	.0003	.016	.010
FOHV *	.162	.083	.724	
Levenstein	.0001			
Miller	.00	.891	-.999	-.176
Palmer *	.031	.011		
W-P	.0001	.017	.022	.569
Carnegie		.417		.606
pooled Z **	8.795	4.917	3.356	2.252
pooled significance ***	.0001	.0001	.0008	.0244

Significance level is computed from data which includes groups which had been out of the program longer than indicated, e.g., "immediate posttest" for starred projects includes some groups for whom the test was actually a one-year posttest.

** $Z = \dfrac{\sum z_i}{\sqrt{k}}$ = where z_i = z score for significance level from the ith project's t-test
k = number of significance tests

*** pooled significance = significance level of the pooled Z score, using a standard Z table

Figures compiled by Harry W. Murray, Research Associate, for presentation in his paper at the American Orthopsychiatric Association Annual Meeting, April 6, 1977.

for reading subtests and for the fourth, fifth, and sixth grades. Thus, comparisons for other grades, other tests, and other subtests will have to be developed.

The only data from school records which will be collected by all studies are the subject's present status in school (graduated, dropped out or the grade (s)he is in), whether (s)he has ever been retained or has skipped a grade, and whether (s)he has ever been in special education. Some studies will collect more extensive school record data such as the subject's curriculum track, school grades, records of suspensions, etc.

Analyses of Original Data

Preliminary analyses of the original data already have been performed in Ithaca using a variety of techniques and approaches. Generally, it may be concluded that these analyses have confirmed what the original researchers have shown in their individual analyses: that significant differences between experimental and control subjects are found at immediate post-test and that these differences persist for up to three years after the termination of the intervention. (In most cases three years was the maximum number of years in which succeeding post-tests were administered.) More detail and explanation of this analysis will be present by Harry Murray in a paper at the American Orthopsychiatric Association meeting in New York City in April. The attached Table I is drawn from that analysis. It must be remembered that this analysis is performed by number of years following termination of the program. Therefore, for the infant studies such as Gordon's, Levenstein's, and Gray's Family-Oriented Home Visitor Program, the age of the child at the last post-test is somewhat younger than that of the children at post-test for the preschool programs.

Results of an analysis by this author, also to be presented at AOA, show significant differences between experimental and control groups through age five for children in infant programs, and through age seven for children in both child-oriented (center-based) and combination child-and-parent-oriented programs (home visits and a center program.) The significance levels among the three groups of programs indicate that greatest differences were found for parent-oriented (or infant programs), next greatest for combination programs, and next for child-oriented (center-based) programs. Results of these analyses are presented in Table II.

Analyses of the follow-up data will begin in early April. As parent and youth interviews are already being received in

Table II.   Analysis of Covariance: Differences Between
             Experimental and Control Subjects on Stanford-
             Binet IQ Scores, Controlling for Pre-Test IQ

Child-Oriented Programs at Age 7

Factor	DF	Mean Square	F	P
Stanford-Binet Pre-test IQ	1	30846.141	308.461	.001
Treatment	1	401.437	4.014	.043
Residual	356	100.00		

Combination-Parent-Child-Oriented Programs, At Age 7

Factor	DF	Mean Square	F	P
Stanford-Binet Pre-test IQ	1	12968.285	99.268	.001
Treatment	1	1059.600	8.111	.005
Residual	301	130.639		

Child-Oriented Programs At Age 6

Factor	DF	Mean Square	F	P
Stanford-Binet Pre-test IQ	1	31678.949	306.005	.001
Treatment	1	569.995	5.506	.019
Residual	368	103.524		

Combination Parent-Child Oriented Programs At Age 6

Factor	DF	Mean Square	F	P
Stanford-Binet Pre-test IQ	1	12458.918	101.038	.001
Treatment	1	2848.001	23.097	.001
Residual	308	123.309		

Table III. Mean Differences on Stanford-Binet IQ Scores
Between Experimental and Control Subjects in
Parent-Oriented Programs

At Age 5

	N	Mean Stanford-Binet IQ	Standard deviation	t	P
Control	58	90.293	12.926	-4.46	<.001
Experimental	194	100.201	15.366		

At Age 4

	N	Mean Stanford-Binet IQ	Standard deviation	t	P
Control	70	90.985	13.236	-3.84	<.001
Experimental	205	99.278	16.332		

At Age 3

	N	Mean Stanford-Binet IQ	Standard deviation	t	P
Control	69	91.536	10.794	-2.95	<.003
Experimental	215	97.190	14.690		

the Consortium office these will be analyzed first.   School
record data and achievement test scores are anticipated next,
with treatment of WISC and WAIS scores projected for late
spring.

The participants in this study believe that these individual studies and the Consortium effort constitute a major
national resource.   The compilation and analysis of this data
can provide a unique empirical base both for further applied
research in child development, and for improvement of public
programs for young children and their families.   The persistence, willingness, and cooperation of the individual investigators have been the major factors in the implementation and
continuation of the study, and the assurance that it will
become a significant contribution to the field of child
development.

A Review of
Head Start Research
Since 1969

Ada Jo Mann, Adele V. Harrell and Maure Hurt, Jr.

Introduction

The Head Start program, since its inception in 1965, has involved thousands of children and millions of dollars. As with any innovative program of this magnitude, there is a body of research dealing with the complex issues involved.

The need of evaluators and researchers for ready access to this ever-growing body of Head Start research literature has led to the development of this document which addresses the impact of Project Head Start on three critical constituencies: the child, the family, and the community.

Impact Questions

Important questions of continuing interest that have been asked about the impact of Head Start center around three subjects, the child, the family, and the community. The child as the primary recipient of Head Start services, is by far the most frequent focus of the majority of the research. Child-focused research on the cognitive, social, and physical aspects of development is predominant in the literature. Studies of the impact of Head Start on the family and the community, although not as well researched as the child-impact studies, are still of major interest.

This document reviews the literature and briefly summarizes the findings relating to the following issues:

1. What is the impact of Head Start on child health?

2. What is the impact of Head Start on the social development of the child?

3. What is the impact of Head Start on the cognitive development of the child?

4. What is the impact of Head Start on the family?

5. What is the impact of Head Start on the community?

The collected literature was reviewed for findings, positive or negative, related to the identified questions. Reports prior to 1969 were not included because earlier research syntheses[1] have reviewed those studies. Summaries of each report found to include relevant findings are presented in Section III. These summaries were condensed into brief presentations of major findings relating to each question (Section II). The next step was to examine the nature and extent of the research on each topic area. Finally, a commentary on the extent of the research on these questions was prepared (Section I).

Data Sources

The Social Research Group has over the last year been collecting reports on research on Head Start for the purpose of reviewing them for findings relevant to policy formulation.

The following sources were used to identify Head Start literature: computer searches of the ERIC system, the PASAR system of journal articles maintained by the American Psychological Association, the Medlars system of references to medical journals, the Libcom system of references to Library of Congress entries, Dissertation Abstracts, the National Technical Information Service (NTIS) system of research reports, the Social Science Citations references to journal article citations, the Smithsonian Science

---

[1] Excellent summaries of earlier Head Start research include:

Data, Lois-ellin. A report on evaluation studies of Project Head Start. A paper presented at American Psychological Association Convention, 1969.

Grotberg, Edith. Review of research, 1965 to 1969, Project Head Start. Washington: Office of Child Development, 1969.

Stearns, Marian S. Report on preschool programs: The effects on disadvantaged children and their families (final report). Office of Child Development, 1971.

White, Sheldon H., et al. Federal programs for young children: Review and recommendations: Vol. I-III, 1973 the Huron Institute.

Information Exchange of on-going research, and the New York
Times Information Bank on articles in 60 business and polit-
ical news magazines and newspapers. In addition, the Bates
Bibliography of Head Start Research, the Congressional
Information Service Index and miscellaneous publications were
used.

The documents were obtained in microfilm, microfiche,
and hard copy, when necessary. As the documents were collected, they were annotated, indexed, and placed on file for
ready access. These documents are available for use by the
research community.

Paper Organization

The remainder of this chapter provides the following
information:

1. Brief "capsule" statements of findings in certain
   crucial program impact areas with lists and description of the relevant references.

2. A discussion of the sources, nature and extent of
   the Head Start literature identified to date.

3. A set of summaries of the findings of studies in
   each of these topic areas.

I. Summary of the Findings and Extent
of Research in Selected Areas

A. What impact does Head Start have on the cognitive development of children?

....*Does participation in Head Start produce gains in intelligence?*

Yes.   The majority of studies showed improvements in performance on standardized tests of intelligence or general ability.

....*Does participation in Head Start produce gains in academic achievement?*

Yes.   Studies reported that Head Start participants performed equal to or better than their peers when they began regular school and there were fewer grade retentions and special class placements.

....*Does participation in full year Head Start programs produce significant gains in cognitive development?*

Yes.   Studies reported that Head Start was effective in preparing children for later reading achievement and intelligence was improved.

....*Does participation in summer Head Start programs produce significant gains in cognitive development?*

No.   The majority of research revealed that children who participated in short term programs did not achieve significant gains.

....*Does one program approach produce more significant gains than another?*

No.   In aggregate the programs produce gains, but no one program or group of programs seems to be superior to another.

Twenty-seven studies were identified which investigated the impact on the cognitive development of children participating in some type of Head Start program. (Summer, Full-year, Planned Variation, Home Start) The majority of these (12) were dissertations which usually involved small samples derived from single Head Start sites.

Five studies examined program effects for single or small groups of Head Start sites. An additional eight of the 27 studies were national evaluations with large, national samples, including reports on Home Start and the Parent-Child Center program, and four reports which examined the effects of Planned Variation. Two studies looked at the effects of Head Start in a particular city. The remaining study was a review of the effects of preschool programs. The following is a list of those studies which included findings on the impact of Head Start on the cognitive development of participanting children.

Barber, Adeline Zachert. A descriptive study of intervention in Head Start. Dissertation Abstracts International, 31 (08-A), 3986, 1971.

Barrett, William J. The effect of Head Start experience on deprived groups: Administrative implications. Dissertation Abstracts International, 28 (9-A), 3400, 1968.

Beard, Helen Marie. The effects of Project Head Start attendance on school readiness. Dissertation Abstracts International, 27 (8-B), 2767, 1967.

Bickley, Marion Thornton. A comparison of differences in selected educational characteristics among culturally disadvantaged children who attended Project Head Start, culturally disadvantaged children who did not attend Project Head Start, and children who are in grade one. Dissertation Abstracts International, 29 (4-A), 1032, 1968.

Bissell, Joan S. Implementation of planned variation in Head Start I. Review and Summary of the Stanford Research Institute Interim Report: First year of evaluation. April 1971 (DHEW Publication No. OCD-72-44).

Burden, Tobi LaBlanche Moss. Changing parent attitudes and improving the intellectual abilities of three-year old, four-year old, and five-year old children through participation in a Home Start program. Dissertation Abstracts International, 34 (11-A), 7037, 1974.

Cain, Glen G. and Barnow, Burt S. The educational performance of children in Head Start and control groups. Final Report. University of Wisconsin, Madison, Wisconsin, 1973.

Chaplan, Abraham A. & Platoff, Joan. Preschool child development program (Head Start) in disadvantaged areas of New York City--Summer 1976. Evaluation of New York City Title I Educational Projects, 1966-67. Center for Urban Education, New York, N.Y. (ED 094 882), microfiche.

Costello, Joan & Benstock, Eleanor. Review and summary of a national survey of the Parent-Child Center program. August, 1970.

Dellinger, Harry Vaughn. A study of the effectiveness of a summar Head Start program on the achievement of first grade children. Dissertation Abstracts International, 32 (9-A), 4832, 1972.

Featherstone, Helen. Cognitive effects of preschool programs on different types of children. Huron Institute, August, 1973.

Grindheim, Rose Voetmann. A comparative study of Head Start programs. Dissertation Abstracts International, 31 (10-A), 3267, 1974.

Hartford moves ahead: An evaluative report. Head Start child development, 1973-74. Hartford Public Schools, Hartford, Connecticut.

Himley, Oliver T. A study to determine if lasting educational and social benefits accrue to summer Head Start participants. Dissertation Abstracts International, 28 (5-A), 1621, 1967.

Home Start evaluation study. Final Report: Findings and implications. High Scope Educational Research Foundation: ABT Associates, Inc., Spring 1976.

Hosey, Harold Ray. Cognitive and affective growth of elementary school students who participated in summer Head Start. Dissertation Abstracts International, 33 (12-A), 6591, 1973.

Hulan, John R. Head Start program and early school achievement. The Elementary School Journal, 1972, 73 (2), 291-94.

Jackson, Dollie Joyce. A comparison of the academic achievement in grades two and three of children who attended an eight-week and an eight-month Head Start program. Dissertation Abstracts International, 31 (4-A), 1512, 1970.

Larsen, Janet Seger. A study of the intelligence and school achievement of children previously enrolled in Project Head Start. Dissertation Abstracts International, 31 (3-A), 1014, 1970.

Larson, Daro E. Stability of gains in intellectual functioning among white children who attended a preschool program in rural Minnesota. Final report. 1972 (ED 066 227).

Lewing, Harold F. An evaluation of a summer Head Start program. Dissertation Abstracts International, 30 (10-A), 4191, 1970.

Scruggs, Allie W. The effect of the Fall River and Lowell Head Start programs on behavioral characteristics associated with lower socioeconomic class preschool children. Dissertation Abstracts International, 32, (4-A), 1949, 1971.

Shipman, Virginia. Disadvantaged children and their first school experience: ETS-Head Start longitudinal study. Preliminary description of the initial sample prior to school enrollment. Summary report, 1971.

Stanford Research Institute. Implementation of planned variation in Head Start: Preliminary evaluations of planned variation in Head Start according to Follow Through approaches (1969-1970), May, 1971.

Stearns, Marian S. Report on preschool programs: The effects on disadvantaged children and their families. Office of Child Development, 1971.

The impact of Head Start: An evaluation of the effects of Head Start on children's cognitive and affective development, executive summary, June, 1969. Westinghouse Learning Corporation; Ohio University.

Weisberg, Herbert I. Short term cognitive effects of Head Start programs: A report on the third year of planned variation, 1971-1972. Cambridge: Huron Institute, June, 1974.

B. What impact does Head Start have on the social develop-
    ment of children?

   ....*Does participation in Head Start produce gains in
        self-concept?*

        No.   The majority of studies did not show a posi-
               tive impact on the self-concept of partici-
               pants except in conjunction with a high degree
               of parent participation.

   ....*Does participation in Head Start have a positive
        impact on achievement motivation?*

        Maybe. The studies on the impact of Head Start on
                achievement motivation have conflicting find-
                ings.

   ....*Does participation in Head Start have a positive
        impact on social behavior?*

        Yes.   Several studies have found that despite vari-
               ations among Head Start programs, it can be
               said that Head Start does positively contri-
               bute to the development of socially mature
               behavior.

   ....*Does participation in Head Start have a positive
        impact on child socialization?*

        Yes.   The majority of studies concluded that Head
               Start facilitates child socialization.

Sixteen studies were identified which examined the impact
of participation in Head Start on the social development of
children. Seven of these studies were dissertations which
involved small samples of children usually drawn from a
single Head Start site. Two other studies examined the effects of parent participation on social developing using children drawn from twenty Head Start sites. One study looked
at program effects of Planned Variation on social development and another investigated the effects of Home Start in
this regard. Another reported on selected aspects of child
development using data derived from two national samples of
full-year Head Start participants. Two literature reviews
were examined for program impact; one on longitudinal studies
and another on evaluation studies. One study observed the
social behavior of 500 disadvantaged children most of whom
were Head Start participants and another study examined the

personality traits and intellectual development of 82 children in six Head Start programs.

The following is a list of those studies which included findings on the impact of Head Start on the social development of participating children.

Benson, Gerald P. & Kuipers, Judith L. Personality correlates of intellectual performance among Head Start children, 1974.

Bromley, Kathleen C. MIDCO Educational Associates, Inc., Non-technical report: Investigation of parent participation in Head Start, 1972.

Custer, Dorothy M. Comparison of fifth year pupils having continuing intervention programs and those without such assistance on certain achievement, adjustment and motivation measures. Dissertation Abstracts International, 32 (8-A), 4237, 1972.

Datta, Lois-ellin. A report on evaluation studies of Project Head Start. Paper presented at the American Psychological Association Convention, Washington, OCD, 1969.

Emmerich, Walter. Structure and development of personal social behaviors in preschool settings, November, 1971.

Home Start evaluation study--Interim Report VI: Program analysis; summative evaluation results; cost-effectiveness analyses. High Scope Educational Research Foundation: ABT Associates, Inc., March 24, 1975.

Hosey, Harold Roy. Cognitive and affective growth of elementary school students who participated in summer Head Start. Dissertation Abstracts International, 33 (12-A), 6591, 1973.

Howe, Alvin Edward. A comparison of parents' and teachers' perceptions of Head Start and non-Head Start students. Dissertation Abstracts International, 32 (01-A), 68, 1970.

McGee, Grace Ann. An evaluation of the effects of the Bessell-Palomares Human Development Program on five year olds in an Appalachian Head Start class. Dissertation Abstracts International, 32 (8-A), 4329, 1972.

MIDCO Educational Associates, Investigation of the effects of parent participation in Head Start. Final technical report, September, 1972.

Phillips, Clyde K., Jr. A comparative study of the effects of a Head Start Follow Through program and a kindergarten program upon the cognitive abilities and self-concepts of children from low socio-economic environments. Dissertation Abstracts International, 32 (7-A), 3629, 1972.

Research Triangle Institute, Final report: A report on two national samples of Head Start classes--some aspects of child development of participants in full year 1967-68 and 1968-69 programs. Durham, N.C., December, 1972.

Ryan, Sally, Ed. Longitudinal evaluations, Volume I: A report on longitudinal evaluations of preschool programs. DHEW publication No. (OHD) 74-24.

Smith, Marshall S. Some short term effects of Project Head Start: A preliminary report on the second year of Planned Variation, 1970-71. Cambridge: Huron Institute, August, 1973.

Thursby, Marilyn Pearcy. Effects of Head Start and Follow Through on dependency striving, dependency conflict, and autonomous achievement striving. Dissertation Abstracts International, 32 (2-A), 801, 1971.

Washington, Dorothy Jean. The relationship of the self-concept and other predictive variables to academic readiness of kindergarten and Head Start enrollees. Dissertation Abstracts International, 35 (5-A), 2557, 1974.

C.   What impact does Head Start have on the families of par-
     ticipating children?

   ....*Does Head Start have a positive impact on the atti-
      tudes of parents toward their children?*

     Yes.   The majority of studies report an improvement
            in parenting abilities and approach to parent-
            hood, as well as a satisfaction with the edu-
            cational gains of their children.

   ....*Does Head Start produce changes in parent behavior?*

     Yes.   Some studies report an increase in positive
            interactions between mothers and their chil-
            dren, as well as an increase in parent par-
            ticipation in later school programs.

   ....*Does parent participation in Head Start produce
      positive gains for children and their families?*

     Yes.   However, the research to date has failed to
            identify which kinds of parent involvement
            activities result in the most gain.

     Seventeen studies were identified which included find-
ngs related to the impact of participation in Head Start on
the family. Nine of these studies were dissertations which,
for the most part, examined the effects of parent involvement
or changes in parent attitudes at individual Head Start sites.
One study looked at the program effects of Home Start on the
family. Another study examined the educational aspirations
of parents after their children had participated in a Head
Start program. One researcher investigated the attitudes of
parents during participation in the Parent-Child Centers
program. One national study of the effects of parent participation in Head Start was identified, while another study
looked specifically at the effects of parent participation on
the achievement of their children. One researcher discussed
the efficacy of a specific parent training model.

     The following is a list of those studies which were
identified as having findings relating to the impact of participation in Head Start on the family.

Bissell, Joan S. Implementation of planned variation in Head
Start I. Review and summary of the Stanford Research Institutes interim report: First year of evaluation. DHEW Publication No. OCD-72-44, April, 1971.

Bromley, Kathleen C., Ed. MIDCO Educational Associates, Inc.; Non-technical report: Investigation of parent participation in Head Start, 1972.

Burden, Tobi LaBlanche Moss. Changing parent attitudes and improving the intellectual abilities of three-year old, four-year old, and five-year old children through participation in a Home Start program. Dissertation Abstracts International, 34 (11-A), 7037, 1974.

Carrier, Bruce & Holmes, Monica. Clustering and the selection of a representative sample for a study of the impact of the national program. Center for Community Research, March, 1972.

Grindheim, Rose Voetmann. A comparative study of Head Start programs. Dissertation Abstracts International, 31 (10-A), 3267, 1974.

Home Start evaluation study, final report: Findings and implications. High Scope Educational Research Foundation: ABT Associates, Inc., Spring, 1976.

Jacobs, Sylvia Helen. Parent involvement in Project Head Start. Dissertation Abstracts International, 31 (4-A), 1649, 1970.

Kinard, Jesse Edward. The effect of parental involvement on achievement of first and second siblings who have attended Head Start and Follow Through programs. Dissertation Abstracts International, 35 (09-A), 5914, 1975.

Lewis, Cornell Theodore. A study of various factors in Head Start and Title I programs in twenty school districts. Dissertation Abstracts International, 32 (01-A), 129, 1971.

Morris, Vivian D. Factors related to parental participation in project Head Start. Dissertation Abstracts International, 34 (08-A), 4576, 1974.

Payne, James Simeon. An investigation of the effect of a training program designed to teach parents how to teach their own Head Start children. Dissertation Abstracts International, 31 (11-A), 5890, 1971.

Project Head Start: Achievements and problems. Office of the Comptroller General of the United States, May 20, 1975, MWD 75-51.

Weld, Lindsay Ann.   Family characteristics and profit from Head Start. Dissertation Abstracts International, 34 (03-B), 1172, 1973.

Williams, Leslie Rowell.   Mending the hoop: A study of roles, desired responsibilities and goals for parents of children in tribally sponsored Head Start programs. Dissertation Abstracts International, 36 (03-A), 1361, 1975.

Willmon, Betty.   Parent participation as a factor in the effectiveness of Head Start programs. Journal of Educational Research, May, 1969, 9, 406-410.

Wohlford, Paul.   An opportunity in community psychology: Psychological services in Project Head Start. Professional Psychology, 1972, 2, 120-128.

Wolotsky, Hyman, et. al. Career development in Head Start. Bank Street College of Education, New York, Career Development Training Program, 1970, V. C26.

D.   <u>What impact does Head Start have on the community?</u>

....*Does Head Start play a role in influencing changes in community institutions?*

<u>Yes</u>.   A national survey of communities with Head Start programs identified institutional changes in all the communities investigated.

....*Does parental participation in Head Start relate to increased community involvement?*

<u>Yes</u>.   The research revealed that parents were more likely to experience increased total involvement over the period that their children were in Head Start and that this was likely to continue after their children entered regular school.

Only three studies were identified which spoke to the issue of Head Start's impact on the community. One was a national survey of Head Start centers. Another was a national survey of the impact of the Parent-Child Center programs and the third investigated the effects of parent participation in Head Start.

The following is a list of these studies:

<u>A national survey of the impacts of Head Start centers on community institutions</u>. Kirschner Associates, Inc.: Albuquerque, N.M., May, 1970.

Costello, Joan & Binstock, Eleanor. <u>Review and summary of a national survey of the Parent-Child Center program</u>. August, 1970, Yale Child Study Center.

MIDCO Educational Associates. <u>Investigation of the effects of parent participation in Head Start, final technical report</u>. September, 1972.

E.   What impact does Head Start have on child health?

    ....*Does participation in Head Start have a positive impact on the health of children?*

> Yes.   The research revealed lower absenteeism, fewer cases of anemia, more immunizations, better nutritional practices and, in general, better health among children who had participated in Head Start.

Six studies were identified with findings relating to the impact of Head Start on the health of participating children. One of these was a dissertation which compared the health status of a small sample of Head Start and non-Head Start children. Another study looked at the incidence of anemia among Head Start children. Two studies reviewed the program effects of the Parent-Child Centers program; one study examined the effects of the Health Start program on its participants and another reviewed findings from the Home Start evaluation study.

The following is a list of these studies.

Costello, Joan & Binstock, Eleanor. Review and summary of a national survey of the Parent-Child Center program, August, 1970.

Geesaman, Patricia Louise. The health status of Project Head Start children and non-Project Head Start children from the same socioeconomic level. Dissertation Abstracts International, 31 (9-B), 5453, 1971.

Holmes, Monica; Holmes, Douglas; Greenspan, Dorie & Tapper, Donna. The impact of the Head Start Parent-Child Centers on children: Final report. Center for Community Research, December, 1973.

Home Start evaluation study. Final report: Findings and implications. High Scope Educational Research Foundation: ABT Associates, Inc., Spring, 1976.

Mickelson, Olaf, et. al. The prevalence of anemia in Head Start Children. Nutrition evaluation, 1968-1969. Merrill Palmer Institute, Detroit, Michigan: Michigan State University, East Lansing, Michigan, Head Start Evaluation and Research Center, 1971.

Vogt, Leona & Wholey, Joseph. Health Start: Final report of the evaluation of the first year program. The Urban Institute, Spetember 29, 1972.

TABLE I

Research on the Impact of Head Start
By Year and Topic Across Subject Area

	Cognitive Development N=27	Social/Emotional Development N=16	Family Impact N=17	Community Impact N=3	Child Health N=6	TOTAL N=59
			Research Topic			
Year of Report						
Prior to 1970	5	1	1	0	0	7
1970	4	1	2	2	1	8
1971	6	2	3	0	2	12
1972	3	6	3	1	1	12
1973	3	2	1	0	1	6
1974	4	3	3	0	0	8
1975	0	1	4	0	0	5
1976	2	0	0	0	1	1
Type of Report						
Dissertation	13	7	9	0	1	27
National Eval.	8	6	4	3	4	18
Literature Rev.	1	2	0	0	0	3
Other	5	1	4	0	1	11

II. Summary of the Nature and
Extent of Head Start Research

A total of fifty-nine research reports were identified
that contained findings related to the impact issues
described. Table I summarizes the sources and dates of these
research reports by topic area. The topic areas are not
mutually exclusive: six reports addressed two questions,
while two reports addressed three questions. The Total Col-
umn in Table I presents the number of reports without overlap.

Dissertations, numbering 27, were found to be a good
source of information for research on Head Start that has not
been widely disseminated. While dissertations were the only
type of report to have findings indicating no impact as shown
in Table II, those that did find positive impact did so in
areas that corroborated the evidence of other research findings. The "no impact" dissertations were most noticeable in
research on the family and on social/emotional development,
topics which are known to be difficult to measure. On the
other hand, the failure of the other types of literature to
report no impact could result in part from the lack of
interest in publishing no impact findings and in part from
the wealth of evidence provided by the wider range data collected in larger studies which yielded positive findings.

Dissertations and national evaluations differed greatly
in their approaches. The dissertations tended to have smaller
samples, usually from one or only a few Head Start sites.
They also typically evaluated only one aspect of Head Start.
In contrast, the national evaluations generally examined a
broader range of questions, used larger samples and a wider
selection of sites. Twelve of the national evaluation reports,
primarily those associated with the Home Start and the Planned Variation studies, looked at outcomes in terms of specified or differential inputs (services) while only three dissertations did so. However, six of the dissertations examined the long term (after two or more years of Head Start)
effects of the program, while only three of the national
evaluation reports did so. It is important to point out that
the unit of this analysis is the report and that several
reports result from each national evaluation while each dissertation reflects a separate research effort.

Table I also reflects the difficulties encountered in
attempting to obtain reports from the most recent research.
Our search source for documents was existing data systems
such as ERIC, and a noticeable time lag between publication
and inclusion in such systems has been observed.

Table II

Head Start Research Findings
by Type of Report

RESEARCH TOPIC

TYPE OF REPORT	Cognitive Development N=27		Social/ Emotional Development N=16		Family Impact N=17		Community Impact N=3		Child Health N=6		Total N=59	
	Positive Impact	No Impact	Positive Impact	No Impact	Positive Impact	No Impact	Positive Impact	No Impact	Positive Impact	No Impact	Positive Impact	No Impact
Dissertation	8	5	2	5	4	5	0	0	1	0	15	13
National Evaluation	8	0	6	0	4	0	3	0	4	0	25	0
Reviews	1	0	2	0	0	0	0	0	0	0	3	0
Other	5	0	1	0	4	0	0	0	1	0	11	0

The most serious gap that was observed was the failure of most of the research to evaluate Head Start as a comprehensive services program. Often a narrow definition of objectives was used which failed to look at the "total" program. In particular, program goals concerning child health and community change were overlooked.

Within the topics frequently addressed, the research often omitted dimensions of crucial importance to policy formulation. Only one study was found that looked at cost or cost/benefit of the program. The precise program inputs were specified in only sixteen reports, leaving many questions of differential implementation unanswered. Finally, only seven reports looked at long term effects of Head Start-- a question that will become of increasing importance as Head Start enters its second decade.

III.   Summaries of Individual Study Findings[*]

A.   *What impact does Head Start have on the cognitive development of children?*

Perhaps the most controversial evaluations of Head Start have focused on its impact on the cognitive development of the child.

Intelligence Gains

Stearns, in a review of studies on the effects of pre-school programs on disadvantaged children and their families reported that the majority of studies showed improvement in performance on standardized tests of intelligence or general ability.

Scruggs measured the effectiveness of Head Start programs in influencing the cognitive development of 42 disadvantaged four year olds and found that both groups made significant gains on a number of variables including intellectual functioning, control of aggressive impulses and auditory discrimination. The greatest gains were seen in the results of the administration of the Stanford-Binet Intelligence Scale. Scruggs concluded that the Head Start program objective of influencing IQ level was supported.

Similarly, Barrett, using the Stanford-Binet Intelligence Scale to measure the cognitive gains of 65 children over a nine-month period, reported that a significant number of participants did show progress at the .01 level and that the whole group achieved a mean gain of 5.62 points. The deprived group demonstrated a higher increment of gain than the control or norm group. The deprived group also achieved a gain in their scores on the Caldwell Cooperative Preschool Inventory.

Larson investigated the degree of stability of significant gains made in intellectual functioning by a group of children who attented Head Start and two groups who did not attend preschool programs. The data collected after first grade showed nonsignificant differences between performance levels in intellectual functioning.

---

*References for the studies underlined in this section can be found in the annotated Bibliography available from the authors.

Academic Achievement

In a study of the gains in academic achievement and social development of 248 children participating in Head Start programs in Hartford, Connecticut, it was found that the Head Start participants started out with an 18 month deficit in language development for their age norm. However, they improved on an average of 13 months after participation in an eight-month program. It was also reported that the Head Start children did better than their peers when they began regular school and there were fewer grade retentions and special class placements among former Head Start pupils.

Hulan in his comparison of 80 Head Start and 240 non-Head Start children found that the results of the Stanford Early School Achievement Test showed that the economically disadvantaged children who participated in Head Start demonstrated achievement equal to that of their more affluent counterparts from the same neighborhoods.

Larsen, in an evaluation of the effect of Head Start on the reading achievement of 25 children found that the program had been effective in preparing children for later reading achievement and the durability of the effect was demonstrated over a three year span.

In a report of findings after one year of the implementation of planned variation in Head Start, Bissell noted that participating children improved in performance on measures of cognitive functioning and academic achievement more than could be attributable to expected maturational patterns in low income children.

In a summary report of the Educational Testing Service Head Start Longitudinal Study of 1,800 children in four poverty areas, Shipman noted that the children demonstrated a greater ability in understanding language than in using it. It was speculated that basic language comprehension may be relatively unaffected by environment; however, this does not seem to be the case with language usage. Shipman reported that the measures of school-related skills, cognitive style and self-concept were difficult to interpret because of their inconsistency from site to site.

Full Year Versus Summer Program

Since the Westinghouse study there has been continued interest in the differential effects of full year (eight months) programs versus summer (eight week) programs. Jackson evaluated the effects of Head Start on the second and third grade academic achievement of four groups of children who previously had participated in Head Start. The groups consisted of (1) lower class children who had been in an eight week summer Head Start class, (2) middle class children who had been in a summer Head Start program, (3) lower class children who had been in an eight-month Head Start program, and (4) middle class children who had been in an eight-month private kindergarten. The study revealed no significant differences between groups in overall achievement as measured by the California Achievement Tests. However, significant differences were detected among groups in specific cognitive skills: the eight-month Head Start groups did significantly better than the eight-week groups on math fundamentals, while the eight-week middle class group scored higher on language usage than the eight-month lower class group.

Barnow has devised a framework for analyzing the effects of Head Start on cognitive development through reanalysis of the Westinghouse data and development of a linear model of "educational production function." The results of his reanalysis showed that both summer and full year programs were effective for white children from mother-headed families, but ineffective for white children from two-parent families. For black children Barnow found that participation in Head Start programs produced a five point gain in IQ when tested in first grade; however, by second and third grade no gains were retained. This study revealed no difference in effects between participation in full year or summer programs for either race.

In another reevaluation of the Westinghouse data using new evaluative procedures, Cain produced findings generally compatible with the original study. He concluded, however, that in general Head Start programs did not emphasize a cognitively oriented curriculum, but rather the emphasis was on delivery of comprehensive services and parental involvement.

In contrast to the findings on the effects of full year programs, the majority of the research which evaluated the effects of summer programs revealed that the children who participated in these short term programs did not achieve significant gains in cognitive skills. Bickley investigated selected characteristics during grade one of children who had attended a summer Head Start program to determine its effect on their reading achievement. Children who were disadvantaged, but who did not participate in Head Start and children who were not disadvantaged were also investigated. No significant differences in reading readiness scores were found as measured by the Durrell Analysis of Reading Difficulty and the Reading Readiness instrument. However, the overall

achievement of the Head Start group was not as great as that
of the group which was not culturally disadvantaged. On the
other hand, the Head Start group did perform better in the
area of oral language than the non-Head Start culturally
disadvantaged group.

Lewing evaluated a summer Head Start program in rural
Illinois by analyzing differences between 87 participants and
73 non-participants using the Primary Reading Profiles and
found no differences between groups on reading achievement.
Hosey compared the long-range academic achievement and self-
concept difference of fourth grade children who participated
previously in a Head Start summer program with a group of
children who were eligible, but who did not participate. He
found that the academic achievement of the Head Start group
was not higher than the control group, nor were the intelligence scores as measured by the Kulymann Finch Intelligence
Tests. The attendance records were similar and no overall
statistical differences were shown.

Similarly, Himley tried to determine if lasting social
and educational benefits accrued to culturally deprived children as a result of their having participated in a summer
Head Start program. Administration of the Metropolitan Readiness Tests revealed no lasting benefits in reading readiness,
number readiness, vocabulary development or social maturity.
Dellinger also found that attendance in a Head Start summer
program was not related to subsequent improved performance on
the Metropolitan Readiness Tests.

In contrast to these studies, Beard found that a group
of 68 children enrolled in a summer Head Start program
improved significantly as measured by the Peabody Picture
Vocabulary Test, the Goodenough-Harris Drawing Test and the
Gesell Development Designs instrument, while the scores of
the non-participating control group remained the same except
on the Vineland Social Maturity Scale. Chaplan, as well,
found that 54% of the teachers interviewed for a sample of
170 randomly selected children felt that participation in a
summer program had adequately prepared the children for
entrance into kindergarten.

Comment

The cognitive gains in intelligence and academic achievement identified as associated with participation in Head
Start (Scruggs, Barrett, Hulan) do not appear to be significantly associated with the summer programs. The period of
intervention must be longer to have enduring effects as

documented by other findings such as those cited in impact on
social development.

Program Approaches

One problem encountered by evaluators of Head Start has
been the difficulty in aggregating the varied program
approaches together for investigation. Several studies have
examined the effects of individual Head Start programs. Planned Variation was an attempt by the Office of Child Development to compare a variety of programs for disadvantaged preschool education.

Featherstone investigated whether different kinds of preschool programs would have differing cognitive effects on
different kinds of children at eight Project Head Start Planned Variation sites. From an analysis of data generated during the first two years of Planned Variation, Featherstone
concluded that there is no one approach which will work for
all children.

In an overall evaluation of eight Planned Variation programs, the Stanford Research Institute found that Head Start
did change the classroom performance of participants as
measured by the Preacademic Skills Test Battery more than
could be expected through normal maturation. It was also
found that, in general, Planned Variation Head Start was
slightly, but not significantly, more effective than the regular Head Start programs, i.e., most children (79.83%) in
Planned Variation programs gained over two standard score
points on the cognitive and preacademic measures. A comparison of the various curricula suggested again that no one approach was more effective than another. The data also
revealed that Head Start seems most effective with the children who need the most help. Overall, Head Start was found
to be associated with significant and substantial effects on
the cognitive growth of children.

In a report on the short term cognitive effects of Head
Start, based on data collected during the third year of
Planned Variation, Weisberg found that both Planned Variation
and regular Head Start participants performed better than
controls on the following cognitive tests: Preschool Inventory, Wide Range Achievement Tests and the Peabody Picture
Vocabulary Test. However, there were no overall differences
between Planned Variation and regular Head Start program effects. The results were quite homogeneous and no one program scored above average in effectiveness on all measures.

Another programmatic approach to Head Start goals was the Home Start program designed to offer children eligible for Head Start and their parents, the same kinds of benefits and stimulations as Head Start, but in a home setting. High Scope Educational Research Foundation reported that in the area of school readiness, the Home Start children, after 7 months, were significantly above the controls as measured by the Preschool Inventory, the DDST Language Scale and the child talk score from the 8-Block Task. At 12 months the PSI was the only single school readiness measure to differentiate the groups, but when all four outcomes were analyzed simultaneously, a significant difference was found favoring the Home Start children. Burden investigated whether there were any changes in mothers' attitudes toward their children or in the children's measured intelligence. Administration of the Hereford Parent Attitude Survey revealed no change in the mothers' attitudes and the Peabody Picture Vocabulary Test scores showed no differences in the children's intellectual growth. However, the tests were administered at the beginning and end of a four month period.

Costello, in an analysis of 34 Parent-Child Centers serving 1,818 families (2,585 children), found that eight centers emphasized a cognitive stimulation approach and 22 centers offered a general developmental approach. The data indicated that no one approach produced better results than another.

Grindheim evaluated the effectiveness of a task-oriented Head Start program using the Metropolitan Readiness Tests and compared the results with those of children attending a traditional nursery school type Head Start program. She found that there was little difference in the effects of the two approaches.

Barber investigated the effects of a program of home intervention which was designed to supplement the regular Head Start program by using paraprofessionals to assist parents in providing intellectual stimulation for their children. The sample included 198 full year Head Start children in three urban and two rural centers. It was hypothesized that the child's performance on various cognitive tasks would be improved after this interaction with his parents as measured by the Peabody Picture Vocabulary Test, the Deal-Dickerson Measure of Logical Expression and the California Test of Personality. The data revealed that the motivation of parents to assist their children was positively related to the child's performance on the above measures of learning skills.

Comment

Participation in Head Start in its many forms relates positively to gains in cognitive skills among the children. The differences in gains among the program approaches are not a major factor influencing the gains.

B.   *What impact does Head Start have on the social development of children?*

> The data pertaining to this question suggest that
> no single answer is possible and that certain pro-
> gram contents, parental roles, and other variables
> will influence the Head Start child's gains in
> this area.

Self-Concept

Washington compared the self-concept of a group of 46
Head Start students of low SES and a group of 46 private non-
disadvantaged kindergarten students, using the Thomas Self-
Concept Values Test. Self-concept was not found to correlate
significantly with group membership, even though the groups
differed markedly in social class background, IQ level, and
amount of preschool experience. The same was true for values.
Moreover, self-concept factors were not related to the reading readiness of either group.

In two additional studies it was found that Head Start
participation did not affect gains in the positive self-
concept of participants. Hosey assessed the positive self-
concept of a group of 24 disadvantaged students who had
participated in a summer Head Start program and a group of
24 first grade students from the same school who had been
eligible for Head Start the preceding year when no program
was available. No significant differences between the two
groups were found either on positive self-concept or any of
six self-concept factors measured by the Piers-Harris Children's Self-Concept Scale. In a study conducted by Phillips
90 pupils from a nine month Head Start program were assigned
to a Head Start/Follow Through program and 75 pupils from the
former program were assigned to a kindergarten program. The
two groups of pupils did not differ in the degree to which
self-concept had improved six months later, as measured by
the Personal Worth subtest of the California Test of Personality.

On the other hand, Custer did find indications that
self-concept had been enhanced in a group of 90 black fifth
grade children whose participation in a Head Start program
was followed by four years of additional intervention programs. The girls of this group were higher in the composite
self-concept factors of esteem, social interest, complexity
of self, identification with friends, and preference for
friends than the girls of a control group of 90 black fifth
grade children from a neighboring county who had been eligible for Head Start but had not been provided with a program.

The Head Start group boys differed from the control group boys only in showing greater preference for their mothers. There were no differences for either sex in the factors of individuation, realism, identification with mother, father, or teacher, or preference for father or teacher.

In the MIDCO investigation of the impact of the participation of parents in Head Start programs on their children, the social development of children was found to be related to the pattern of parent participation. Parent participation in Head Start was categorized as high or low participation in decision-making roles and in learner roles. However, high parental participation in decision-making roles was associated with increased identification with significant others among the children in the program. When looking at the individual children within sites, children of parents highly active in learner roles think of themselves as happier, but have lower preference for friends than children of parents highly active in decision-making roles. Writing on the same study, Bromley found that the self-concept of children was enhanced in centers with high levels of participation in one or both parent roles and that the children of parents high in decision-making roles and learner roles had a better self-concept than the children of parents low in both parent roles.

Comment

One weakness of most of these studies in directing policy is first that membership in a Head Start program was assumed to represent treatment and no other measures of treatment input or variability were used. Thus, with so little information on what other "treatments" were operating, it is difficult to suggest program modifications to improve performance. It is possible that variability in treatments or lack of inputs is the cause of the no impact findings.

Custer's study suggests, as have many other studies, that long term and continuing intervention are necessary to produce significant changes, though again the specific program inputs associated with these gains are not specified.

Only the MIDCO study attempts to associate program characteristics with outcome. However, the problem here is whether the parent participation aspects of the program structure affected the child's self-concept or whether, in fact, the relationship between improved child self-concept and parent participation in certain aspects of the Head Start program resulted from basic prior differences among Head Start parents in their own competence and parenting skills. If one is willing to assume that the parental participation roles in Head Start is causally related to improved self-esteem of the children, then the policy implications of the study are that efforts should be made to increase parent participation in the programs in all roles and most particularly in active decision-making roles. Further examination of the effectiveness of parent participation in learning roles as an effective means of improving parenting skills and, therefore, child self-esteem, is certainly suggested.

Achievement Motivation

Large-scale evaluations of early Head Start programs have yielded possible inconsistent results concerning achievement motivation. A study conducted by Research Triangle found that the gains of participating children in achievement motivation were greater than expected at usual maturational rates, using the Gumpgookies test, as well as the Behvior Problem Scale, a Motivation Problem Scale, and a Feeling of Inadequacy Scale from the Inventory of Factors Affecting the Stanford-Binet. These gains were not related to child age and sex, nor to parental characteristics such as aspirations, expectations, amount of reading to the child, number of visits to the classroom and child rearing practices. However, differences related to ethnicity do appear.

In another study of achievement, Thursby has attempted to replicate Beller's finding that preschool experience raises autonomous achievement striving and lowers dependency conflict. The subjects under study consisted of one group of 28 Follow Through children who had had a year of kindergarten prior to first grade, a second group of 59 Follow Through children who had participated in summer Head Start prior to first grade, and a third group of 49 children who were enrolled in regular first grade classes and who had had no preschool experience. Beller's instrument was replaced by an observational procedure. Data obtained through this procedure provided little support for the earlier predictions.

Comment

The impact of Head Start on achievement motivation has not been clarified. Increases in achievement motivation appear to occur, but the durability of such gains has been challenged.

Social Behavior

Several studies attempt to relate Head Start program inputs to social-personal behaviors of the children. Smith used the fall-spring scores on the Preschool Behavior

Observation System of 16 children to study the programmatic
approaches of Planned Variation in Head Start. No evidence
for hypothesized relationships between the social-personal
behaviors, including self-esteem, interpersonal skills, and
autonomy of the children and their learning environments was
obtained. The comparison is among Head Start programs, however, not between them and control groups not receiving Head
Start. On the other hand, McGee exposed nine Head Start pupils to Human Development Program materials for 28 weeks of
training. Although no systematic changes were found in personal adjustment and social adjustment, the children did show
improvements in self-awareness, effectiveness, awareness of
others, interpersonal comprehension, and tolerance; those
changes were considered significant, indicating positive
relationship between program content and child behavior.

In evaluating Home Start, Deloria found significant differences in the social-emotional development of children after
12 months in the program with the Shaffer Behavior Inventory
and the Pupil Observation Checklist Sociability Scale. In
addition, Howe reported that as late as second grade, both
parents and teachers rated children who had attended Head
Start more mature socially on the Vineland Social Maturity
Scale than similar children who did not attend Head Start.

Comment

Thus, while variations among Head Start programs may or
may not affect social behavior differently, it can be said
that Head Start does positively contribute to the development
of socially mature behavior.

Child Socialization

Head Start may facilitate child socialization. In one
review of Head Start evaluation studies, Ryan has observed
that Head Start boys were more mature than non-Head Start
boys both before and after kindergarten. In another review
of Head Start evaluation studies, Datta has concluded that
interactions with children from other ethnic groups and
verbal interactions with children and adults are increased
for Head Start participants. These gains appear to be independent of age, I.Q. level, and program content. Several
other studies of the social development of Head Start children have indirect implications for program planning, but no
findings relevant to evaluating program impact.

Benson and Kuipers have examined the relationship between various personality dimensions and intellectual development in 82 Head Start children. As hypothesized, extraversion,

task orientation, general adjustment, and peer adjustment were found to correlate positively with intellectual development; distractibility and introversion were found to correlate negatively with intellectual development and hostility and considerateness were found not to correlate with intellectual development. These findings were unaffected by the factors of sex, ethnicity, and economic status. The study concludes that Head Start programs should, therefore, attempt to create situations that require self-initiating, exploratory, persistent, and independent activity on the part of the child.

For example, Emmerich rated 500 urban preschool children on the basis of observations made in "free play" periods under minimally structured conditions. The majority of the children were black and enrolled in Head Start. It was found that 18 constructs of the personal-social behaviors of these children could be organized into the three dimensions of Extraversion vs. Introversion, Warmth vs. Hostility, and Task vs. Peer Orientation. Most global changes observed during the year were in a direction consistent with accepted socialization goals, with the majority of children showing effective adaptation to the basic requirements of a preschool environment. Writing on the same study, Ward observed further evidence for the presence of a three-dimensional configuration in the personal-social behaviors of Head Start children. No significant relationships were found between these behaviors and self-regulatory behaviors. It was concluded that young socioeconomically disadvantaged children achieve an organization of personal-social behaviors comparable to that of middle-class children, even though they have not yet achieved such comparability in the cognitive domain.

No attempt was made to compare the Head Start children to untreated disadvantaged children or to middle class children, nor was the study designed "to determine whether subgroup differences and transformations within subgroups take on a different pattern when independent variables associated with the child's home experiences and classroom environment are considered." Thus, no program evaluation was presented nor intended.

Comment

In summary, Head Start factors associated with social and emotional gains appear to be parent participation (MIDCO), continuing intervention (Hosey, Custer) and curriculum focused intensely on social skills (McGee). As a whole, Head Start contributes to the social development of the participating children. One question not addressed was to what extent the improved social development is associated with later success in school.

C.   *What impact does Head Start have on the families of participating children?*

> The question of the impact of Head Start on the
> families of participating children is crucial. Head
> Start was, from the beginning, designed to help the
> disadvantaged child and his family overcome the
> obstacles that could hinder the child's later suc-
> cess. The intent was and is to assist the disad-
> vantaged family in the task of child rearing. The
> program has attempted through involving the parents
> in a wide variety of participatory roles to support
> and encourage them in making maximum use of their
> own talents and available community resources for
> their children's benefit. To accomplish this goal,
> the participation of the parents in Head Start pro-
> gram activities has been considered essential.

Parent Attitudes

Parental reaction to the Head Start program has been
overwhelmingly positive. The Bank Street study found that
the greatest source of parent satisfaction was the educational gains parents observed in their children, followed by
self-reported feelings of increased understanding of the
child and improved parenting abilities as well as increased
feelings of self-confidence and coping ability. Similar
results were found by Carrier and Holmes in their study of
the attitudes of parents participating in the Parent and
Child Cneters. Ninety-five percent of the interviewed parents stated that the program had positive effects, either
educational or on parental self-confidence. A majority
reported gains in their approach to motherhood. Similar parental attitudes are reported by the MIDCO and Bromley in an
extensive study of parental involvement in Head Start. However, Jacobs' study of a Head Start project in Austin failed
to find changes in maternal optimism, aspirations for the
child or child-rearing practices. Burden, in looking at Home
Start, also reported no change in maternal attitudes associated with being in the program. These study results appear
to be the exception, rather than the rule.

Changes in Parent Behavior

Although Head Start has generally had a positive effect
on parental attitudes, has it positively affected the parents'
behavior towards their children or in their use of community
resources? Bissell reported a significant increase in Head
Start mothers' verbal communication with their children and
in their praise of them in a learning task using the Hess and

Shipman Eight Block Sort Task. Lewis cites an increase in extent and kind of parental participation in the later school programs of children who attended Head Start, resulting either from changed parental behaviors or changed school practices that encourage such involvement, or both. However, the evaluation of Home Start did not find significant lasting gains in the mother-child relationship as measured by the Mother Behavior Observation Scale, nor in maternal teaching behaviors or family-community involvement. The study did find a significant increase in the presence of playthings for children in the home which could indicate an enrichment of the home environment.

When comparisons were made between Home Start and regular Head Start participating parents differences were found primarily on home environment variables. At both 7 and 12 months, Home Start mothers reported teaching more elementary reading and writing skills to their children. At 20 months Home Start mothers reported they more frequently let their children "help" with simple household tasks.

Parent Participation

Projects can provide opportunities for involving parents in program planning and operation, in classroom activities, in support activities, and in work with their own children in cooperation with Head Start staff. The nature and extent of parental participation in eight surveyed Head Start projects were reported in excerpts from the GAO Report to the Congress, Project Head Start.

In addition, Willmon found that reading scores and active parent participation in a summer Head Start program were highly and positively associated, although prior parent attitudes and behavior are probably the causal factor. While Kinard found both the extent of parent participation and the length of exposure to a comprehensive program (Head Start versus Head Start and Follow Through) related significantly to child achievement as measured in second grade on the Metropolitan Achievement Tests.

Studies of particular parent training programs showed mixed results, depending on the model tried. In a policy study, Morris was unable to identify any factors that could be adjusted by the program personnel that significantly affected the parent participation in one Head Start project. This line of inquiry should be pursued in an attempt to identify which kinds of parent involvement activities result in the most gain to the children and families and the ways in which parent participation can be increased.

Who benefits

The question of which families benefit the most from
Head Start was asked by Weld who compared the residual gain
scores on the Preschool Inventory, the Peabody Picture Vocabulary Test, the Birthday Test, the Stanford-Binet Intelligence
Scale and several measures of child behavior to a number of
family characteristics. Perception of the value of education,
provision for the child's immaturity and suppor for individ-
uality were characteristic of families whose children gained
the most from Head Start. Positive attitudes regarding the
importance of education were found by Grindheim to be more
characteristic of Head Start families than similar families
who did not have children enrolled.

Comment

While the actual extent of parent participation in Head
Start has not been documented adequately, it is clear that
high parental participation is associated with gains both on
the part of the child and the parent. Improved documentation
of parent participation and diversified opportunities for
participation by working mothers and fathers should be
investigated. No studies addressed the question of how many
mothers entered the workforce as a result of having Head
Start available to them.

D.   *What impact does Head Start have on the community?*

Project Head Start has a number of stated goals designed
to improve the opportunities and potential of disadvantaged
children. It was anticipated that one related outgrowth of
the program would be its impact on the community and various
community institutions.

The results of a national survey by <u>Kirschner Associates</u>
of the impacts of Head Start centers on community institutions
for the period from July 1968 through January 1970 were published. The purpose of the survey was to obtain a greater
understanding of Head Start's role in influencing changes in
community institutions. It was found that institutional
changes consistent in direction with Head Start goals and
philosophies were identified in all of the communities investigated. A total of 1,496 changes were identified in 58 communities studied. Of the total of 1,496 changes, 1,055 were
educational in nature and 441 were classified as health
related. Table III displays the number of institutional
changes in each of four categories.

In the summary of a national survey of the Parent-Child
Center Program conducted in 1970, the program's impact on
local communities was noted. It was found that in many communities, particularly in rural areas, the Parent-Child
Centers gained high visibility and were effective in bringing
together a variety of agencies which serve children and
families.

In a study conducted by <u>MIDCO Educational Associates</u> in
1972, investigating the effects of parent participation in
Head Start, it was found that parent involvement in Head Start
may have been related to community involvement. There were
some indications that Head Start programs where parents were
highly active may have helped to develop increased feelings
of community involvement. The parents were more likely to
experience and feel increased total involvement over the
period that their children were in Head Start, and this was
likely to continue after their children enter school.

The following is a summary of the <u>MIDCO</u> findings which
reflects the relationship between parent participation and
Head Start's impact on community institutions:

1.   Both the greatest number of changes and the more
      significant changes were reported in centers rated
      high in both decision-making and learner activities.

TABLE   III

Number of Institutional Changes
In Each of Four Categories

Category of Institutional Change	Frequency	Percent of Total
Increased involvement of the poor with institutions, particularly at decision-making capacities	305	20.3
Greater employment of local persons in paraprofessional occupations	51	3.4
Greater educational emphasis on the particular needs of the poor and of minorities	747	50.0
Modification of health services and practices to serve the poor better and more sensitively	393	26.3
Totals	1,496	100.0

2. The centers which reported the most significant kind of institutional changes were those where decision-making was the stronger of the two roles.

3. There was a direct relationship between the extent of parent participation and the ability of parents at a center to recall and document changes.

4. Significant and important institutional changes appeared to be associated with a number of factors:

    a. Parents who were interested in the welfare of their families.

    b. Head Start staffs who provided opportunities for parent involvement in decision-making and learner roles.

    c. Staffs who provided continued support and encouragement.

    d. Community leaders who were responsive to the needs of low income families.

    e. Federal and state policies and funding which provided a support base and climate conducive to bringing about change for the benefit of low income families.

E.   *What impact does Head Start have on child health?*

It is widely accepted that good health is necessary for the optimal development of children. A major concern of Head Start has been to provide preventive health care, to screen, diagnose and treat health problems, and to promote good health care practices and services. However, little research has been done to document the extent to which needed services have been provided and the impact of Head Start health care on the physical well being of children.

Geesaman compared a group of 31 children chosen from a group of 203 children who had attended a Head Start program in Bloomington, Indiana, with a control group of students at the same school matched by paternal occupation. She found that absenteeism was lower among students previously enrolled in Head Start than among the control group, although the reported immunization levels and cases of reported childhood disease did not differ. This may suggest that alternative means of access to health services were available to the non-Head Start children, and that factors other than health, such as improved adjustment to school and higher levels of maternal employment could explain the lower absenteeism of the children who had attended Head Start.

Health Needs

The health needs of Head Start children and the health care alternatives available to them have not been thoroughly documented. Mickelson looked at the nutrition status of Head Start children and found that among 77 Head Start children in Pontiac, Michigan, anemia was not as prevalent as expected. Sixty percent of the tested children fell in the high range of hemoglobin levels. In addition, the height of these children was found to be normal. The author cautions that such findings may differ by geographic location.

Health Programs Related
To Head Start

The success of one special focus program of Head Start, the Parent-Child Center (PCC) in improving child health has been evaluated. Costello found that infants in the Parent-Child Centers showed substantial gains in the first year of enrollment on both the mental and motor scales of the Bayley Infant Development. Holmes found that the Centers positively affect both the number of immunizations received (especially in urban areas) and the dental care received. The Centers did not appear to affect nutrition practices or prenatal and well baby clinic visits.

In evaluating Health Start, <u>Vogt</u> found that 78% of the children enrolled in 1973 received medical exams, with 24% needing treatment. Fifty-six percent of those who needed treatment received it. Similarly, 42% of the enrollees received dental exams, with 44% needing dental care and 38% of these children receiving it. The study further examined cost efficient methods of delivering health care.

In the <u>Home Start Evalution</u> study mothers of participating children reported that they believed that their children were receiving better medical and dental care as a result of the Home Start program.

Comment

This meager array of studies emphasizes the need to identify specifically the health problems of disadvantaged children by geographic location, to identify alterantive sources of health care, and then to examine the impact of Head Start in alleviating the health problems of enrolled children.

Long-Term Gains from Early Invention

An Overview of Current Research

Bernard Brown

In the eleven years since the founding of Project Head Start, the effectiveness of early childhood programs for disadvantaged children has been the subject of intense public as well as academic debate. Does early intervention produce lasting gains in intellectual development? The papers presented here have attempted to answer this question through the analysis of longitudinal experiments.

New data is now available from a series of longitudinal studies begun in the sixties. The children in the original preschool programs (who have now passed the third grade) have been carefully monitored and tested from their initial entry into the program to the present. They are now old enough for their scores on achievement and IQ tests to be reliable. The preceding papers present a massive set of findings on the efficacy of early intervention.

The longitudinal data is buttressed with information from other research and evaluation studies which have accumulated at a rapid pace over the past four years. In addition, methods of statistical analysis have become more sensitive and sophisticated, necessitating reanalysis of older data. Thus, the time has come to review the status of our knowledge about early intervention.

Although achievement and IQ scores continue to be used to gauge program effectiveness, the validity of these measures is widely suspect as unrepresentative of children's basic competence.

In addition to reviewing the preceding papers, this paper reviews some striking evidence of gains outside the cognitive area. It also addresses the question of why the weight of evidence seems to have shifted so strongly in favor of preschool programs and what this implies for the future of child development and children.

Positive Findings Reported in This Volume

The paper by Goodson and Hess (Chapter 3) reviews the effects of 28 programs which train parents to teach school-related skills to their young children. Nearly all of these compensatory education programs produced immediate gains in IQ. Follow-up testing when treatment and control children were in elementary school showed that program children retained an advantage in IQ and school achievement.

The children studied by Seitz, et al. (Chapter 4) were enrolled in Head Start and then in Follow Through. When these children were given continuing attention as they developed, there was no "fade out" of intellectual gains for those who were ahead of controls at the end of the program. In fact, there appeared to be "sleeper effects" which showed up several years after the end of the program. Of particular interest in Seitz's study is the finding that, while children performed well after they left Follow Through, they had a lesser liking for school. This may be a consequence of their awareness that public schools provide a less positive experience than Follow Through.

Palmer (Chapter 2) reviewed ten major early intervention programs (including both center and home based programs) involving over 3,000 children who were followed longitudinally through third grade and beyond. Several years ago, it was noted that there was some decrease over time in initial IQ gains obtained immediately following the end of the interventions. However, Palmer found that when achievement and IQ were later measured in the third grade and beyond (ages for which better IQ measures were available) the children's performance was higher than would have been expected without the intervention.

The studies reviewed in Palmer's paper are the major longitudinal studies which are being independently analyzed by the Developmental Continuity Consortium at Cornell. The results of their first analyses (Hubbell, Chapter 6) appear to confirm Palmer's findings.

The review of the Head Start literature by Mann, Harrell and Hurt of the Social Research Group at George Washington University contains an annotated bibliography of over 700 studies of Head Start and Early Intervention (which is included in the appendix to this volume). Of particular interest is their analysis of the evaluations of Head Start's long and short term impact (Chapter 7). The "score" of positive impacts to "no difference" findings in their review was 49-13. But a closer look at the 13 "no difference" findings reveals that they were doctoral dissertations which were restricted to a few local centers and included relatively small numbers of children. It is difficult to see how any of these 13 investigations could have had sufficient statistical power; that is, their small numbers did not permit them to conclude that positive impacts were not overlooked. Thus, in Mann's analysis, the proper "score" is 49-0.

Other Positive Findings

Cataldo (1977) has just completed a dissertation on a follow-up study of Irving Sigel's Early Education Project at SUNY, Buffalo. The treatment subjects were ahead of their control and peer comparison classmates in reading and mathematics after five years.

A number of other long-term positive impact findings have not been referred to in the preceding papers. These include the studies of Woolman (1977), Fowler (1972), Herzog (1972), Lysiak (1972), Hodges (1967), Sprigle (1972), White (1973), and Heber (1972, 1974).

The Developmental Continuity Consortium

The principal major longitudinal studies of early intervention begun in the sixties now have extensive data on these children. In order to overcome the problems associated with statistical significance and small numbers, an attempt is being made to analyze these data by pooling the data from all of the studies and using a common set of measures for another round of data collection (Hubbell, Chapter 6).

The analyses are part of a project conducted by a consortium of 12 principal investigators who have conducted longitudinal research on early childhood education projects for low income families. The consortium is chaired by Dr. Irving Lazar of Cornell and is currently engaged in two interrelated efforts to provide better information on the actual effects of preschools on low income children. These two efforts are:

(1) pooling the original longitudinal data collected by the individual investigators, and

(2) collecting current year follow-up data from all projects in identical format for use in both pooled and separate analyses. Harry

> Murray and Ruth Hubbell have just fin-
> ished two papers analyzing IQ and family
> characteristics.

By pooling the significance level of the post test scores
(treatment group scores minus control group scores), Murray
found the pooled significance level for eight of the studies.
For the immediate post test, a positive impact was found with
a pooled significance level of less than .0001. At one year
after preschool, the pooled significance level was .0001. At
two years it was .0008, and at three years it was .024. The
initial mean gains showed some decline but continued positive
impacts were found through age 10. To say the least, these
are impressive first findings.

While much work remains to be done by the Developmental
Continuity Consortium, their analyses will probably become
the definitive work on the effectiveness of early intervention. The analytic techniques they develop will probably influence the design of longitudinal studies of early intervention for the next decade.

Impact on Personal-Social Development,
Grade Retention and Placement in
Special Education Classes

There are five studies which have reported that early
intervention has led to marked reductions in the number of
children placed in special education classes or retained in
grade. Ira Gordon (Guinagh, 1976) found that 10% of his
treatment group were placed in special education classes as
against 30% of his controls. Goodstein (1975) found that a
significantly smaller percentage of former Head Start children than non-Head Start children had been placed in special
education classes or retained in grade even though there was
no significant difference in his sixth grade academic achievement data. Shipman has reported similar findings.

Palmer found that 42% of his control group children were
set back in grade one or more years in contrast to only 20%
of the children in his treatment program. In the Perry project, Weikart found that 25% of his control group (97 out of
385 children) required some form of special education or
institutionalized care compared to only 13% of his experimental group.

In her doctoral dissertation, Carol Weber (1975) (an
economist) analyzed Weikart's findings from a financial view-
point. Weikart's children required less costly forms of education as they progressed through school (such as less

special education and institutional care). Weber added this economic benefit to the value of parents' released time while children attended the program and to the increase in the children's projected life time earnings. She found that the <u>annual</u> rate of return on investment from the above benefits was 9.5% of the cost of one year of Weikart's preschool program.

In Lally and Honig's <u>Family Development Research Program</u> a 10-point IQ difference at 36 months favoring the infants in the treatment group became small at 60 months and seems to have disappeared by 72 months. (Their control group, which had higher attrition than their treatment group, had a mean IQ at 72 months of 106.) But the fascinating aspect of the Lally data is their Emmerich Personal Social Scale findings. The Emmerich showed significant differences in favor of treatment children at 60 to 72 months. These children, who had been in Lally's program for five years, were more involved, relaxed, energetic, social, independent, purposeful, affectionate, flexible, friendly--and they laughed and smiled more.

In addition to social/emotional benefits and a reduced need for special education, there are yet other aspects of early intervention which we should consider. We should, for example, ask, as has Gershenson (1977): "How many of these children have entered the child welfare system?" Additionally, we might also ask:

o   Did the intervention help take the parent-child interaction through a critical period?

o   Are we dealing with a preventive program which opens the mother's life space?

o   How many children were saved from placement, child abuse, or neglect?

o   How many dollars were saved from mental health clinics, child welfare institutions, placement out of the mother's home?

o   Should we worry about 10 IQ points or two billion dollars of Title XX funds?

"No Difference" Findings: Are They Valid?

During the past decade, many studies of social programs have suggested that the programs produced no permanent difference in the status of their participants. Repeatedly, the public was told that there was no impact on children from Head Start, better schools, and the like. The Rand Study for the President's Commission on School Finance (Averch, 1971) concluded: "Nothing consistently and unambiguously makes a difference in student outcomes." Jencks (1972) asserted: "No measurable school resource or policy shows a consistent relationship to schools' effectiveness in boosting student achievement." The micro-economists also found negative results on the effect of schooling. This despite the fact that the macro-economist Denison (1962) has credited education with the major contribution to the growth of the U.S. economy. It will be argued below that these studies suffered from a statistical analysis defect. They ignored small cumulative errors. The reason macro-economists have attached such great importance to education and other social programs may be that their mode of analysis integrates the effects of economic factors over decades and even generations.

Consider the basic case of a test of the difference between a treatment and control group. We test the null hypothesis that the means are not different against the alternative hypothesis that the means are different. We make a Type I error when we reject the null hypothesis when it is in fact true. On the other hand, if we accept the null hypothesis (assume there is no difference) when there is in fact a difference, we make a Type II error. Both Type I error and Type II error can lead us to wrong conclusions. Unfortunately, most evaluation technology concerns only significance, which refers to Type I error.

What does a "no difference" finding mean in classical statistics? Most of the "no difference" findings of the past eight years were analyzed by statistical tests of hypotheses which concentrated on Type I error rather than Type II error (see Brewer, 1972). In those analyses which actually addressed Type II error, unreasonably large effects were postulated. The "no difference" findings from social program evaluations were thus focussed on the wrong question.

To the social program evaluator, there is one overriding question: "Did the program work?" It is of little use to him to test the null hypothesis for the purpose of proving that there is no difference. All he can learn is that he did not make a mistake of observation, a Type I error. He may have found no difference only because his instruments were insensitive.

He should ask: "Did the treatment produce a difference greater than a given standard (a specified critical value)?" Now it is no easy matter to set a standard for what constitutes a difference, but easy or not, that is what must be done in order to pose a meaningful question. What the social program evaluator must avoid is the rejection of the alternative hypothesis when it is true. His concern is properly with Type II error. In other words, he has a vital interest in the power of a difference test.

The Westinghouse evaluators of Head Start, in order to insure sufficient test power and significance, assumed large critical values. Had a smaller critical value been chosen, it would have resulted in an insignificant test. The evaluators responded to a natural pressure to come up with highly significant results. The apparatus of statistics was thus inadvertently used to discriminate against the detection of small but important effects.

I suggest that the Westinghouse Report, the Rand Report, the Jencks study and the micro-economic studies all ignored small cumulative effects. It is hard to escape the conclusion that their investigators determined their results by the way they defined their problems. They could not see differences smaller than the differences they assumed.

A New Look at the Westinghouse Report

The most notorious "no difference" finding and the one most often cited as evidence that early intervention does not work is the Westinghouse Learning Corporation evaluation of Head Start (Cicirelli, 1969). Technically it is not a negative finding because the study did find that the full year Head Start programs actually had a positive impact. However, the eight week summer Head Start programs were found to have a negative impact on the achievement levels of the Head Start children. Smith and Bissell (1970) and Campbell and Erlebacher (1970 a, b) have addressed the biases in the sample selection and the defects in the design and analysis of this "ex post facto" study.

The Westinghouse report was controversial from the start. "Shortly after the results were announced, Robert Finch, the Secretary of Health, Education and Welfare, announced that the study 'contained insufficient facts and the data was sloppy'; Dr. William Madow, the chief statistical consultant to the study publicly withdrew his name from the report; the White House defended the results of the study; and the directors of the summer Head Start programs (involving over a million children) were given the option of shifting their funds to full-year programs" (Smith, 1970, p. 52).

Barnow (1973) reanalyzed the data. He concluded that the summer programs were effective for certain groups of participants by use of a covariance analysis.

Rindskopf (1976), allowing for unrealiability in a constructed measure of SES, reanalyzed the summer Head Start data and found significant positive effects for reliability estimates as low as 0.3.

In a recent reanalysis, Jay Magidson of Abt Associates (1977) reexamined the Westinghouse summer data. Using a path analysis procedure, Magidson corrected for SES bias in the comparison groups and found that there was indeed a <u>positive</u> impact from the summer program. There may be other ways to do the path analysis and better sets of assumptions, but at this point the Westinghouse report stands disproved regarding summer Head Start. Westinghouse today must be considered a positive finding.

The Validity of the Studies

The studies presented in the preceding papers are noteworthy for their sophistication in design, execution, and analysis. The large scale execution of longitudinal studies with control groups represents a major advance in applied social research. The most impressive aspect of the papers is that such a large number of studies show gains in cognitive development.

Those of us afflicted with critical and skeptical points of view can point out weaknesses in some of the studies. We can question the selection methods, the designs, the sampling procedures, and the statistical analyses.

To discover the most likely source of bias running through all of these studies, I suggest that we look at the men and women who ran the programs. They are, all of them, people who love and care and intend the best for children and who are intensely sympathetic to the plight of the disadvantaged child. They are believers who want early intervention to succeed. On that score they all stand, if you will, indicted.

But a bona fide skeptic is skeptical of skepticism. The possibility of bias is not proof of bias. I judge these investigators to be objective scholars driven to perform the most exacting and careful (I would even say over-conservative) analyses. They believe that truth is on their side and that honest, objective inquiry will prove the benefit of early intervention.

If they have indeed biased their studies they have done so in a most individualistic manner. The data trends shoot off in all directions. Depending on the particular study,

sample attrition can raise or lower gains. The selection procedures sometimes favor the control over the comparison group.
In addition, these investigators have demanded exacting standards of impact. It is noteworthy and their data and analyses are public. As the studies have progressed, the findings
have been regularly reported in the literature. In particular
the longitudinal study participants, by sharing their data,
have laid themselves bare. They will be second guessed for a
decade.

While any one of the studies cited may be faulted, there
are just too many for all to be flawed in the same direction.
To be sure, most and maybe all can be improved, but that is
not the question before us. We are judging probable program
impact, not giving grades for pretty experiments.

Lessons From The Longitudinal Studies

We have learned--and relearned--a great deal from these
studies: that child development is a continuous process;
that early intervention is most effective when it makes a
lasting change in a child's environment; and that the duration of intervention is also a critical factor for which the
rule seems to be "the longer the better" (subject, of course,
to cost/benefit analysis). On this latter point, Dr. Seitz's
work suggests that the combination of a year of Head Start
followed by several years of Follow Through is more effective
than a single year of Head Start alone. This finding is con-
sonant with simulation studies of early intervention (Brown,
1972).

The investigations cited in this volume comprise a convincing demonstration of the value of longitudinal designs
for early intervention experiments. This approach is neither
quick nor cheap; nor is it easy. But it is an excellent
investment of our resources, principally because in the long
run it is sure. And, it is a rich source of understanding
about the intervention process. Longitudinal studies have
begun to show a high degree of sophistication and longitudinal methodology seems destined for a period of rapid advancement.

Another convincing demonstration which has come out of
these studies is the value of the "laboratory" study as an
adjunct to program evaluation. Few efforts at evaluating
social programs are adjudged to yield much useful information.
This comes about in part because human service programs such
as Head Start and Follow Through are established to help
people not to answer some theoretical questions about program
effectiveness. Reliable scientific analyses require precise

deliberate preparation, rigid experimental design, scientific objectivity and careful control of program activities, all of which are often inimical to bureaucratic imperatives and human service goals. In the university-based "laboratory" study, social science and human service can be effectively combined. The wisdom gained from these small scale experiments may then be generalized to larger social programs. In contrast, the direct evaluation of large social programs has many times resulted in uninterpretable data because in large programs the caregivers' first concern is invariably to help the children they serve.

The Road Ahead

While the results reported here are enormously encouraging, we should not let the hard work we have done obscure the hard work we have yet to do. Social scientists need better tools: tests which go beyond the simplistic assessment of cognitive gains and truly measure a child's competence in adapting to the world outside the classroom. We need better and more flexible experimental designs and statistical analysis tools. We must find some way around the increasing bureaucratic restrictions and stumbling blocks which delay and weaken our studies and raise evaluation costs.

We must work harder at translating our rapidly increasing knowledge of child development into working programs, new curricula, new materials and new service delivery models. We must individualize our programs so that they meet the needs of every child. We still have much to learn about the role of families and about the impact of family size and birth spacing on children. However, we also have new knowledge which can be translated into programs for children in such areas as: dental, medical, and nutritional services; preventive mental health; social development; and parent involvement. The tremendous strides we have made in the past few years in such fields as psycholinguistics and perception are barely beginning to affect preschool education.

We still have not fully explored the many ways in which Head Start and other early intervention programs can be used to benefit wider and more generalized sectors of our society. Quite often innovative ideas and programs sponsored by the various Head Start programs (which then serve as a laboratory) have broad application. For example, the delivery and financing of children's health services has been improved because of the success of Head Start's innovative health programs. Additionally, the Head Start Performance Standards are an innovation which translates a set of recommended practices into a flexible but enforceable national program.

The Silent Revolution

Since the founding of Head Start, early childhood education in the United States has undergone a quiet but pervasive change; it is now an accepted and functioning institution. The acceptance can be seen not only in the grass roots support for Head Start which sustained it in its years of adversity, but also in the phenomenal rise in nursery schools, preschool programs in the public schools, and quality day care for middle class children. It is evidenced in the plethora of books, records, toys and television programs for preschool children.

In eleven years, an eyeblink in history, Head Start has brought about a silent revolution in children's institutions in the United States. The Head Start center has become an instrument of community change, of family support, of income transfer to needy areas, and of long-term improvement in family health. A two-thousand-year trend of isolation of the public school from community influence and a narrow focus on achievement has been countered by parent involvement and social competency philosophies. Children are respected for the competences that they have rather than those which are demanded of them. Head Start has stimulated an enormous volume of research and debate in child development. No other institution of its size has been so responsive to study or so supportive of research even when the research is critical of the institution.

We are now gathering the first fruits of the longitudinal studies of early intervention, most of which began after the birth of Head Start in 1965. This, in my view, portends a rich harvest. We have some 96 studies: compelling evidence that early intervention works, that the adverse impact of a poverty environment on children can be overcome by appropriate treatment.

With these 96 findings of positive impact, Head Start and early childhood education have passed a milestone. We do not have an airtight case because in the social sciences there are no absolutes. Rather, the terms of discourse about early interventions have been altered. We no longer ask, "Does it work?": Now we ask:

- How does it work?

- For whom does it work?

- How can it work better?

Clearly, social science has progressed. We have learned something new about how to design, implement, and analyze a social experiment. Our poor beleagured Science of Man, with all of its uncertainty and bias, has taken a few steps forward and we are wiser and abler for the effort.

A child of the War on Poverty, Head Start appears to have won a battle. The victory is a tribute to Head Start's staff, the parents who gave of themselves, and the hundreds of dedicated child development specialists who performed these studies. But even more, it is a tribute to a compassionate and caring nation which has given the world a new standard of social progress; a tribute to a nation which is socially creative, which is optimistic, which dares to solve its problems.

(The views and opinions expressed herein are those of the author and do not necessarily reflect those of the Office of Child Development.)

References

Ambrose, A.   Stimulation in early infancy: Proceedings of the Center for Advanced Study in the Developmental Sciences. New York: Academic Press, 1969.

Averch, H., et al.   How effective is schooling: A critical review and synthesis of research findings. Santa Monica: Rand Corporation, 1971.

Barnow, B. S.   The effects of Head Start and socio-economic status on cognitive development of disadvantaged children. Doctoral dissertation, University of Wisconsin, 1973.

Beller, E. K.   Impact of early education on disadvantaged children.   In S. Ryan (Ed.), A report on longitudinal evaluations of preschool programs. Washington, D.C.: Office of Child Development, 1972.

Borden, J. P., et al.   Extended positive effects of a comprehensive Head Start-Follow Through program sequence on academic performance of rural disadvantaged students. Journal of Negro Education, 1975, 44, 149-160.

Brewer, J. K.   On the power of statistical tests in the American Educational Research Journal. American Educational Research Journal, 1972, 9(3), 391-401.

Brewer, J. K.   Issues of power: Clarification. American Educational Research Journal, 1974, 11, 189-192.

Brown, Bernard.   Growth retardation. Doctoral dissertation, The American University, 1972.

Campbell, D. T. & Erlebacher, A.   How regression artifacts in quasi-experimental evaluations can mistakenly make compensatory education look harmful.   In J. Hellmuth (Ed.), Compensatory education: A national debate. Vol. III of the disadvantaged child. New York: Brunner/Mazel, 1970, 185-210.   (a)

Campbell, D. T. & Erlebacher, A.   Reply to the replies.   In J. Hellmuth (Ed.), Compensatory education: A national debate. Vol. III of the disadvantaged child. New York: Brunner/Mazel, 1970, 221-225.   (b)

Carpenter, F. A. A study of the reading achievement of Negro
Head Start first-grade students compared with Negro non-
Head Start first-grade students. Dissertation Abstracts,
1967, 28(7A), 2593.

Cataldo, C. A follow-up study of early intervention.
Doctoral dissertation, State University of New York,
Buffalo, 1977.

Cicirelli, V. G., et al. The impact of Head Start: An evaluation of the effects of Head Start on children's
cognitive and affective development, Vols. 1 and 2. A
report presented to the Office of Economic Opportunity
pursuant to contract B89-4536, June, 1969. Ohio University, Westinghouse Learning Corporation, 1969.

Denenberg, V. H. Education of the infant and young child.
New York: Academic Press, 1970.

Denison, E. C. The sources of economic growth in the United
States and the alternatives before us. New York: Committee for Economic Development, 1962.

Deutsch, M., Taleporos, E., & Victor, J. A brief synopsis
of an initial enrichment program in early childhood. In
S. R. Ryan (Ed.), A report on longitudinal evaluations
of preschool programs. Washington, D.C.: Office of
Child Development, 1972.

Fowler, W. A developmental learning approach to infant care
in a group setting. Merrill-Palmer Quarterly, 1972, 18,
145-175.

Gershenshon, C. Private communication. 1977.

Goodstein, H. A., et al. The prediction of elementary
school failure among high-risk children. Paper presented
at the Annual Meeting of the American Educational Research
Association, 1975.

Guinagh, B. J. & Gordon, I. J. School performance as a
function of early stimulation (Final Report, Grant No.
NIH-HEW-OCD-90-C-638). Institute for Development of
Human Resources, University of Florida, 1976.

Heber, R. T. Progress report (No. 16-P-56811/S-10).
Madison: University of Wisconsin, January 1975.

Heber, R., et al. Rehabilitation of families at risk for mental retardation. Madison: Rehabilitation Research and Training Center in Mental Retardation, University of Wisconsin, 1972.

Herzog, E., Newcomb, C. H. & Cisin, I. H. Double Deprivation: The less they have the less they learn. In S. Ryan (Ed.), A report on longitudinal evaluations of preschool programs. Washington, D.C.: Office of Child Development, 1972.

Hodges, W. L., McCandless, B. R. & Spicker, H. H. The development and evaluation of a diagnostically based curriculum for preschool psychosocially deprived children. Washington, D.C.: U.S. Office of Education, 1967.

Horowitz, F. D. Infant learning and development: Retrospect and prospect. Merrill-Palmer Quarterly, 1968, 14, 101-120.

Illingsworth, R. S. The development of the infant and young child. Baltimore: Williams and Wilkins, 1973.

Jencks, Christopher, et al. Inequality. New York: Basic Books, 1972.

Karnes, M. B., Zehrbach, R. R. & Teska, J. A. An ameliorative approach in the development of curriculum. In R. K. Parker (Ed.), The preschool in action. Boston: Allyn and Bacon, 1972, 353-381.

Keister, M. E. A demonstration project: Group care of infants and toddlers. Final report submitted to the Children's Bureau, Office of Child Development, DHEW, 1970.

Lally, J. R. The family development research program enrichment. (Final Report). College for Human Development, Syracuse University, March, 1977.

Lally, J. R. & Honig, A. S. The family development research program. In M. Day & R. Parker (Eds.), The preschool in action (2nd Ed.). New York: Allyn and Bacon, 1977.

Lewis, E. P. A comparison of the academic achievement of Head Start pupils with non-Head Start pupils. Dissertation Abstracts, 1967, 28(9A), 3368.

Lysiak, F. L. Follow-up research on children who were enrolled in the central cities early childhood program, (Final report). National Center for Educational Research and Development, December 6, 1972, (ED 082 828).

Magidson, J. Toward a causal model approach for adjusting for pre-existing differences in the non-equivalent control group situation: A general alternative to ANCOVA. Abt Associates, 1977.

Magidson, J., Barnow, B., & Campbell, D. Correcting the underadjustment bias in the original Head Start evaluation (Evaluation Research Report No. 2JM). Evanston: Northwestern University, Psychology Department, 1976.

Mann, A. J., Harrell, A., & Hurt, M., Jr. A review of Head Start research since 1969. (Draft). Washington, D.C.: The George Washington University, Social Research Group, December, 1976.

Painter, G. The effect of a structured tutorial program on the cognitive and language development of culturally dis- advantaged infants. Merrill-Palmer Quarterly, 1969, 15, 279-294.

Parker, R. K. (Ed.). The preschool in action: Exploring early childhood programs. Boston: Allyn and Bacon, 1973.

Rindskopf, D. A comparison of various regression-correction methods for evaluating non-experimental research. Doc- toral dissertation, Iowa State University, 1976.

Robinson, H. B. & Robinson, N. M. Development of very young children in a comprehensive day care program: The first two years. Child Development, 1971, 42, 1673-1683.

Shipman, Virginia, private communication, 1977.

Smith, M. S. & Bissell, J. S. Report analysis: The impact of Head Start. Harvard Educational Review, 1970, 40(1), 51-104.

Sprigle, H. Learning to learn program. In S. Ryan (Ed.), A report of longitudinal evaluations of preschool pro- grams. Washington, D.C.: Office of Child Development, 1972.

White, B. L. & Watts, J. C. Experience and environment: Major influences on the development of the young child, Vol. I. Englewood Cliffs: Prentice-Hall, 1973.

Weber, C. U. An economic analysis of the Ypsilanti Perry preschool compensatory education project. Doctoral dissertation, University of Maryland, 1975.

Index

Abelson, W.D., 27, 33
academic achievement, 8, 29,
   74, 80, 93, 94, 113,
   114. *See also* school
   success
achievement striving,
   autonomous, 114
achievement tests, 122, 123,
   169, 170
  scores, 57, 58
adolescence, 79
affectional bonds, 5
age
  at pre-test, 120
  of training, 16, 20
aggression, 114
arithmetic, 19, 20, 28,
   32. *See also* mathe-
   matics
assessment (evaluation),
   18
attendance, school, 81, 83,
   106
attrition, 19, 34, 80, 82,
   83, 87, 89, 121

Bank Street College, 9
Barbrack, 66, 73
Barnow, B.S., 175
basic skills, 103
Bayley Infant Scales, 119,
   120
Beller, Kuno, 22, 33, 111,
   14

Bereiter-Engelmann Curricu-
   lum, 116
bilingual worker, 5
Birmingham Parent-Child
   Development Center, 44,
   57, 71, 72, 74
Bissell, J.S., 175
Brim, O.G., 38, 39
Bronfenbrenner, Urie, 8, 14,
   32, 34
Brookline Early Education
   Project, 3
Brown, Bernard, 4
bulldozer effect, 3

Caldwell's Home Inventory,
   73
California Achievement Test,
   58, 114, 117
Campbell, D.T., 175
career aspiration, 105
Cataldo, C., 171
Cattell Test, 120
center-based programs, 112,
   115
Child Development Associate,
   5
Cicirelli, V.G., 175
cognitive
  development, 1, 129, 130,
     132, 133, 148, 150,
     176
  performance, 18, 21, 26,
     30, 31, 112

Cognitive Home Environment Scale, 73
Coleman, J.S., 41
community, 129, 130, 142, 164
comparison groups, 20
compensatory education, 2, 12, 32, 170
concept
  formation, 12, 21, 113
  training, 17, 115
control groups, 20, 27, 28, 29
Cornell University, 111
crime rates, 11
culturally-different child, 3

Davis, Mary D., 39
delivery system, 112
demographic characteristics, 122
Demonstration and Research Center for Early Education (DARCEE), 26, 116
Deutsch, Cynthia, 111, 113
Deutsch, Martin, 21, 33, 111, 113, 122
Developmental Continuity Consortium, 111, 122, 123, 128, 170, 171, 172
Discovery Program, 115
Dyer, J., 75

early intervention
  different approaches, 111, 112
  economic benefit, 173
  effects on parents, 112, 117, 118
  instilling early self-confidence, 104
early school failure, 104
Early Training Project, 29, 45, 58, 114
ecological intervention, 8
Education Commission of the States, 4, 19, 111

Educational Testing Service, 4
Emmerich Personal Social Scale, 173
Erlebacher, A., 175

fade-out, 103, 170
family, 129, 130, 139, 161, 163
  as change agent, 118
  development, 6
family-centered intervention, 8
Family Development Research Program, 173
Follow Through, 27, 79-108 *passim*, 113, 170, 177
follow-up studies, 111, 123, 125, 171
Fowler, W., 171

Gallagher, James, 3
general information scores, 83, 97, 99, 101, 103, 113
Gershenson, C., 173
Goodson, B.D., 170
Goodstein, H.A., 172
Gordon, Ira, 3, 30, 33, 37, 71, 117, 172
grade level, 105. *See also* retention in grade
  seventh grade performance, 98, 99
  third grade performance, 98
grades (marks), 58, 81, 83, 105
Gray, Susan, 29, 114, 118
Harlem Research Center, 16
Harrell, Adele, 4, 170
Head Start, 2, 12, 27, 34, 35, 79, 80, 81, 113, 116, 122, 170, 173, 175, 178, 179
Head Start Performance Standards, 5
health, child, 129, 143, 167, 168

Heber, R.T., 3, 171
Herzog, E., 171
Hess, Robert D., 4, 40, 41, 170
Hodges, W.L., 171
home-based programs, 5, 112, 117, 119
home environments, changes in, 73, 74, 112
Home Learning Center, 117
Home-Oriented Preschool Education (HOPE), 45, 68
home visiting strategies, 44
Honig, A., 173
housing conditions, poor, 112
Houston Model Program, 5
Houston Parent-Child Development Center, 43, 71, 72, 74
Hubbell, V.R., 171, 172
Hunt, J.M., 3, 41
Hurt, Maure, 4, 170

Illinois Test of Psycho-linguistic Abilities, 113, 116
income levels. *See* low income and middle income
Infant Intervention Project, 43
instruction-to-parents, 65, 68, 69
  specificity in, 68, 69
instrumentation, 121
instrument comparability, 123
intelligence tests, 114
  standardized, 53
  Stanford-Binet, 113, 116, 117, 118, 119, 120, 121. *See also* IQ
interview, 81, 83, 104. *See also* Youth Interview; Parent Interview
intrafamily effects, study of, 43

IQ, 12, 13, 18, 19, 20, 21, 22, 23, 25, 26, 27, 30, 31, 32, 80, 113, 114, 115, 169, 170
  differential effects of programs on, 59
  immediate gains in, 74, 170

Jamison, D., 48
Jencks, C., 41
Jensen, Arthur, 12, 32
Jester, R., 71

Karnes, Merle, 24, 33, 111, 115, 116
kindergarten
  academic, 116
  public, 114

Lally, R., 173
language development, 113
Lazar, Irving, 4, 111, 171
Learning to Learn Program, 47, 55, 57, 59
Leiter International Picture Vocabulary Test, 117
Levenstein, Phyllis, 31, 33, 111, 118
Lilly Endowment(Eli), 9
literacy levels, 2
longitudinal studies, 1, 4, 79, 169, 176, 177
  designs, 172, 177
long-term effects, 53, 79, 98, 169
low educational levels, 112
low income levels, 112
low socio-economic status, 112
Lysiak, F.L., 171

Magidson, J., 176
Mann, Ada Jo, 4, 170, 171
Maternal Teaching Strategy Instrument, 118
mathematics, 83, 97, 98, 99, 103, 113, 116. *See also* arithmetic
Metropolitan Achievement Test, 82, 115

Metropolitan Reading Readi-
    ness Test, 116
Micro-Social Laboratory, 115
middle income children, 81
Miller, Louise, 25, 32, 33,
    75, 111, 115, 116
Milwaukee Project, 3
missing data, 95
Montessori, 26
Mother-Child Home Program,
    42, 55, 58
mother-child interactions,
    6
mother's
  child-rearing concepts, 8
  self-esteem, 117
Mother's Training Program,
    45
Mother Study, First Gener-
    ation, 43
Mother Study, Second
    Generation, 43, 72
motor performance, 18
Murray, Harry, 119, 125, 172

Neighborhood Family Develop-
    ment Center, 9
New Orleans Parent-Child
    Development Center, 45,
    70, 72
Nimnicht, Glen, 3
no difference findings, 171,
    173
non-comparability, sources
    of, 120
nonverbal behavior, 72, 73
nursery school, experimen-
    tal, 114. *See also*
    pre-school

Office of Child Development,
    2, 111
one-to-one instruction, 17

Palmer, F.H., 33, 111, 115,
    170, 172
parent
  attitudes, outcomes in, 70
  education, 38, 84
  involvement, 2, 39

parent, cont.
  surrogates, 8
Parent Attitude Research
    Instrument (PARI), 71
Parent-Child Course, 45, 49
Parent-Child Development
    Centers, 5
parent-child dyad, 112, 117
parent/child interactions,
    immediate outcomes in,
    71
Parent Education Program, 117
  early child stimulation
    through, 44, 55, 65,
    70, 73, 74
parenthood, preparation for,
    5
Parent Interview, 122
parents
  as policy makers, 37
  as supporting resources,
    37
  methods for instructing,
    39. *See also* instruc-
    tion-to-parents.
Parents Are Teachers Too,
    47, 73
parent teaching activities,
    69
  curricular focus, 65
  structure in, 67, 69
parent training programs, 39
  effects of, 48, 69
Peabody Individual Achieve-
    ment Test, 82, 97
Peabody Picture Vocabulary
    Test, 81, 83, 97, 99,
    113, 116, 117, 118, 121
peer pressure, 104
perceptual
  development, 113
  performance, 18, 21
personal development, 172
Piaget, J., 117, 119
pluralistic orientation, 3
pooled significance level,
    172
pooling data, 111
pre-kindergarten, non-
    academic, 116

preschool
  experience, 84
  programs, 1, 114, 169,
    179
Project Early Push, 47, 68,
  74
public schools, 11, 22, 80,
  114

random assignment, 120
reading, 2, 11, 19, 20, 22,
  25, 28, 32, 103, 114,
  116
  comprehension, 83, 97
  recognition, 83, 97
re-awakening effect, 2
receptive language instrument, 118   •
replication waves, 9
research design, 16, 34
retention in grade, 20, 125,
  172
Richmond, J., 2
Rindskopf, D., 176
Royce, Jacqueline, 123

Schlossman, S., 38
school records, 122, 125
school success, 104, 114
  aptitudes for, 114
  attitudes toward, 114.
    See also academic
    achievement
science, 114
Screening Test of Academic
  Readiness, 81
Seitz, V., 27, 33, 170
selection, 16, 34, 83, 84, 87
self-concept, 113
Shipman, V., 2, 4, 172
siblings
  changes in, 73
  number of, 84
Sigel, I., 171
single-model intervention,
  113, 114
Six Hour Retarded Children,
  3
sleeper effect, 2, 99, 103,
  170
Smith, M., 175

social
  behavior, 58
  development, 2, 129, 136,
    137, 149, 155, 158,
    172
social studies, 114
socio-emotional development,
  112, 113, 114
Spanish-Dame Bilingual Education Program, 46
special education assignment,
  125, 172
Special Kindergarten Intervention Program (SKIP),
  45, 68, 73
spelling, 83, 97, 114
Sprigle, H., 171
staffing patterns, 112
Stallings, J., 75
Structured Language Program,
  47, 49, 72
Sunley, R., 38
Suppes, P., 48
System for Open Learning, 3

teacher/parent ratio, 66, 69
Teaching Parents Teaching,
  47, 49
Type I error, 174
Type II error, 174

University of Hawaii Center
  for Research in Early
  Childhood Education, 46,
  67, 70

verbal
  behavior, 72
  interaction, 119
Verbal Interaction Project,
  31, 118
video-tape recordings, 6

washout effect, 2
Weber, C.U., 172, 173
Wechsler Adult Intelligence
  Scale, 122, 128
Wechsler Intelligence Scale
  for Children, 57, 122,
  128

Weikart, David, 28, 75, 111,
    114, 115, 116, 119, 122,
    172, 173
welfare system, child, 173
Wells, S., 48
Westinghouse Report, 4, 79,
    175
White, B.L., 4, 171
Woolman, Myron, 111, 115,
    171

Ypsilanti-Carnegie Infant
    Education Project, 44,
    55, 71, 72

Ypsilanti Curriculum Demon-
    stration Project, 46
Ypsilanti Early Education
    Program, 46, 55, 71, 73
Ypsilanti-Perry Preschool
    Program, 28, 46, 53, 55,
    57, 58, 74, 114, 172
Youth Interview, 123

Zigler, Edward, 2, 4, 111,
    113